THE LALIBELA

HANDBOOK

Damien Pryor

**A guide to the13th century rock sanctuaries
in Ethiopia
Understanding their purpose and meaning**

Also available by this author:
The Great Pyramid and the Sphinx
The Externsteine: Europe's greatest Celtic site
Stonehenge: The essential guide to its purpose and context
The tropical zodiac, its origin and validity; the origin of the zodiac signs

ISBN 9780958134194

CONTENTS

Above the Akeru porch of Biet Maryam:
the spiritual challenge
The Three Beasts: the great catharsis
Lalibela's private contemplation cell
Inside Biet Maryam

Chapter One: General overview of the site

Historical-cultural background

Lalibela is the only site ever built from a cosmopolitan mystical understanding of the Christian religion; as such, it could be called the most mystical of all Christian sites. Most of the monuments here were built in the early thirteenth century, at approximately the same time as the final stage of the great cathedral of Chartres was underway. Lalibela is similar to the great sacred sites of antiquity in so far as it has a mystical language embedded in its structure. Although it is a Christian site, it owes its existence to a strange spiritual experience, similar to those reported from the Mysteries of ancient Greece. The architecture and artworks at Lalibela hint at doctrines found in the ancient Egyptian religion of Osiris and medieval mystical literature.

By the fourth century Christianity had become the State-Church, and had jettisoned all those who were still interested in its own mystical teachings. Church officials forcibly closed down the Hellenistic Mystery centres, and from then on, the building of great sacred sites of an esoteric nature was no longer possible. Consequently in the western world, exploration of mystical themes which interested people in the Grecian Mysteries, came to an end.

These themes typical of the Hellenistic world included the planetary spheres and the zodiac, and the spiritual energies activated in the seasonal cycle of the year. Another theme was the famous 'katabasis' journey, that is the descent into the Underworld, as celebrated in Grecian myths. All such themes were now forbidden by the Church. But it is significant that these subjects were now also of interest to a smaller number of people, than was the case in earlier ages. One exception was the journey of the dead in the spirit realms, now referred to as Purgatory. Rituals for the dead were permitted, but they were re-phrased and incorporated into the new religion.

Throughout a wide area of Europe and the near East, Christendom prospered once Emperor Constantine gave it his official approval. Many sacred sites were being built, but these were sacred to the new state religion, so they were ecclesiastical sites, such as churches, chapels and monasteries. Such sites were not devoted to heretical mystical themes, where the focus was on the possibility to explore the spiritual in the cosmos and how it is linked to the spiritual in the human being. There were still small groups of mystically inclined people in Christendom.

But such people could only gather discreetly and they were always exposed to the risk of being arrested. Hence they lived on the outskirts of society, or in self-supporting larger communities which had a semblance of orthodoxy, but which kept a nervous eye on the Roman Church and its military might.

But there were some other people in the Middle Ages with an interest in esoteric wisdom and in Christianity, who did not live as harassed heretics. Some of the church Orders were more mystically inclined, such as the Cistercians who taught from Chartres cathedral. They carefully integrated their mystical quest into the language of the church, in an attempt to avoid the danger of arrest or torture imposed by the Church-State on such people. Although after some centuries of peaceful co-existence they too were executed by the church.

So, under these circumstances it seems the Christian era did not create an esoteric sacred site, of the kind that could be compared to the ancient sites of the famous Mysteries, such as Eleusis and Ephesus. At least, this was not done, in Europe! It was done however, far away in the deeply Christian land of Ethiopia, at a remote site called Lalibela. Here is to be found the only Christian sacred site that compares, to some extent, to the great ancient sites of antiquity. And as we shall see, its Christianity was heretical by most standards for it had similarities to the sun-god religion of Egypt and elsewhere.

Location and description

Lalibela is an isolated place, a town of perhaps 7,000 people, 640 kms from the capital of Ethiopia, Addis Ababa, on a plateau in the foothills of the Lasta Mountains, at an altitude of 8,500ft (2,630 m). It now has a new section with modern dwellings and hotels; and the old section with traditional grass hut-type dwellings. Until the 1960's the only access to Lalibela was by a three-week trek by mule from Addis Ababa or a four-wheel drive vehicle, carrying its own spare petrol. Twenty years later a better road was made, and in recent years an airport has been constructed. Consequently over the last few centuries, until very recently, few people had been to this remote site, and fewer still had written a substantial report about it. Lalibela was a remote, isolated place in the highlands of Ethiopia. But in modern times it has become accessible.

A stay at Lalibela is becoming comfortable, as the Ethiopian Government has expended considerable effort and funds to facilitate travellers reaching the site. The sanctuary site is divided into two halves, by a narrow (often dry) waterway; the northern and the southern sides. At the beginning of the northern side is where you purchase tickets, for a small charge.

That a site of this complexity and size was built in such an isolated location, with only a village nearby, indicates something significant about its intended usage. It was not meant to be a popular site; it was not designed to encourage large crowds of people. Its log bridges are somewhat dangerous and the maze of tunnels are confronting, if not actually dis-quietening to the visitor, especially those tunnels and hollows in rock walls with skeletons in them. So it appears that its purpose was initiatory and contemplative; its isolation, like that of the Maes Howe site in the Orkneys and the Externsteine in Germany, and many other such sites, was deliberately chosen. A good website for more information about visiting Lalibela is, http://www.tourismethiopia.gov.et/

Ethiopia has a very long and deep Christian heritage. The New Testament itself records in the Book of Acts, (8:26) how an angel arranged for one of the disciples of Jesus, called Philip, to meet a high-ranking Ethiopian man who consequently converted to Christianity; and this happened just a few decades after the death of Christ. There is an implication here that the new religion would soon be taken into Ethiopia, and that this was divine Will. Some of the more valuable, and more mystical Christian writings were preserved carefully in Ethiopia, and had become almost unobtainable elsewhere. See illustration 1 for a diagram giving an overview of the complex arrangement of the site's buildings.

Its Christian towns and monuments were built by the predominating Aksumites or Axum people, a civilisation that arrived in Ethiopia about 500 BC, and became Christian in the 5th century. There are also ancient monuments to be seen from earlier, non-Christian indigenous peoples. So, what is this unusual place all about?

As George Gerster writes it is strangely fascinating place, there is more to it than just a group of churches:

> Let the visitor only subject himself or herself to the shafts and galleries, courts and halls, tunnels, gateways and terraces! No need to pay attention to the tales of secret passages and secret chambers; the labyrinth is labyrinthine enough as it is. Surprises lurk in every corner. Without any warning, the visitor suddenly catches sight of a church below, crouching in the bottom of a pit. Or else, crawling through an insignificant hole in a rock wall, one finds oneself, equally unprepared, at the foot of a church, towering up to heaven. (1)

This site is indeed strangely complex in its design; in fact, its layout defies explanation until its mystical purpose is discovered. See illustrations 2 and 3 to see the complexity of the site, how it incorporates the natural topography, and is riddled with tunnels and trenches. Lalibela's design reflects a mystical and cosmopolitan Christianity, with distinctively mystical tendencies. Consequently, the site was already a venerated pilgrimage place by the 1400's. There is a report from a monk, a certain 'brother Thomas', about his visit in 1523 to Lalibela. He was a missionary and one of the few Europeans of that era to write about Lalibela as a specific place,

> "…where there are 12 churches of canons and a bishop and the tomb of a holy king that works miracles and has the name of "Lalivela"; whither go many pilgrims." (2)

We will look at the structure and position of the monuments, and their placement within the site as a whole, as this is very specifically designed to convey a spiritual message. Each building is called a Biet that means a place of worship, which in the Christian world is called a church, of course.

But here the term sanctuary may be more appropriate at times, as not all the buildings are churches. We note that in some of the buildings there are paintings of animals and various symbols; this is very unusual for Ethiopia, where the Old Testament attitude of not permitting artistic depictions (graven images) was always the rule.

As we explore these questions, we shall see the deeper message of these buildings, and it becomes clear that they must derive from a person who underwent an extraordinary spiritual experience. There are 10 churches or mystical sanctuaries here, and Ethiopian documents written about 250 years after Lalibela life, partly historical partly legendary, do emphasize that they were built as a result of a spiritual experience by this king.

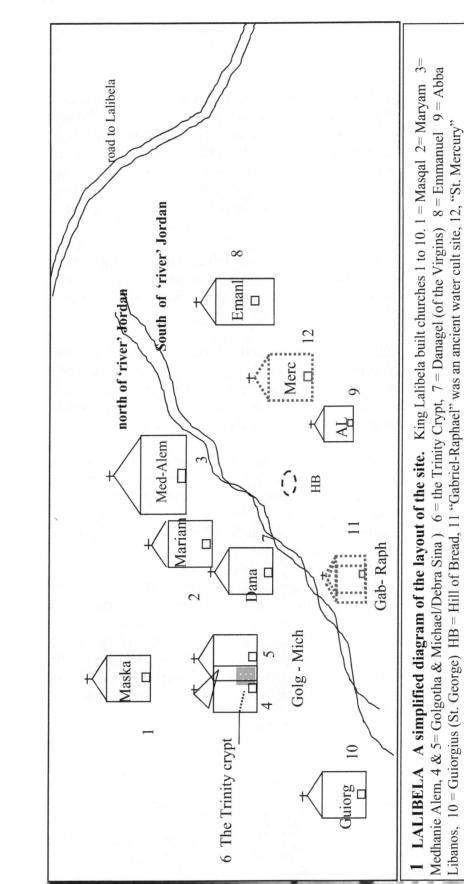

1 LALIBELA A simplified diagram of the layout of the site. King Lalibela built churches 1 to 10. 1 = Masqal 2= Maryam 3= Medhanie Alem, 4 & 5= Golgotha & Michael/Debra Sina) 6 = the Trinity Crypt, 7 = Danagel (of the Virgins) 8 = Emmanuel 9 = Abba Libanos, 10 = Guiorgius (St. George) HB = Hill of Bread, 11 "Gabriel-Raphael" was an ancient water cult site, 12, "St. Mercury"

Travellers' reports from the early 20th century

The first modern report on the churches created by Lalibela was made when Italian forces invaded Abyssinia in 1935, and remained there until 1940. During this time, an Italian archaeological expedition to Lasta in April-May 1939 was led by Prof. A.A. Monti della Corte. Corte was able to get access to Lalibela and investigate all of its churches. The sketches made by Corte, published in the 1940's in Rome, are of great value in understanding the layout of the site.

Possibly the next European to get official access to the churches after Corte (but not all of them) was a British woman, Beatrice Playne, a professional mural painter, in 1945. As her intention was in the best interests of the artworks, the Memhir or senior priest at Lalibela assisted her, and she was allowed to restore some of the old paintings inside the churches.

Beatrice Playne wrote about Lalibela in her book on Ethiopia (St. George for Ethiopia), in the context of searching for old indigenous artworks; she gives a rare glimpse into the life of the people there, prior to its modernization. In the mid-1950s, I. Bidder, wife of the West German ambassador in Addis Ababa, together with three other Germans, visited Lalibela.

She afterwards published a richly illustrated book that was translated into English, and which is valuable for its photographs. Her interpretation of the monuments was refreshingly open-minded, as she looked for evidence of mystical influences, but her conclusions are seriously flawed, due to lack of expertise in the general theme.

A few years after Bidder's visit, another German traveller, H. Pfeiffer visited and was given permission to enter all the buildings, without exception, and to take various photographs. Then in the 1960's the new Memhir, Afe Worq, gave permission to Georg Gerster to take extensive official photos, as the first foreigner after the Italians to do so.

His book has the finest photographs of the site ever taken, but it is long out of print. A small number of other people visited here in the early to mid 20th century. Their reports, printed as small books or articles in literary journals are quite valuable, but now rare, see the Appendix for more about Books on Lalibela.

An overview of the sanctuaries there
The carving of churches out of solid rock underground, with sometimes only one small entrance, would have been a very difficult task. And unfortunately there is no historical information available about the logistics of their construction. Who actually built the site is unknown, it has been rumoured that the stonemasons came from Egypt or even Jerusalem, but various scholars assert that the Ethiopians were quite capable of carving them, just as they built the marvellous buildings elsewhere in Ethiopia, such as at Axum.

The churches are truly extraordinary, they are just not what you expect; they speak of an architectural origin that is right out of the ordinary. They are carved out of the rocky ground, and only dimly illumined by a few rays of sunlight, (so when you visit, a torch is a necessity, although now fluorescent lights have been installed in some buildings). Although constructed as a Christian site, its underlying purpose is to provide a series of solemn sanctuaries, where deeply mystical ideas about Christianity can be contemplated.

All the buildings are positioned in deep trenches, and they are connected by a maze of tunnels, and some have mystical scenes carved on their walls. There is controversy over what influences are discernible in the style of the buildings here. Some travellers argue for a purely indigenous Ethiopian style, others find that some of the monuments here just don't fit the known various Ethiopian styles of architecture.

The churches were made by excavating a trench out of the volcanic rock that forms the ground. A trench was cut around the perimeter of the site and then, standing in the new trench, workmen chiselled into the large block of rock which the trench created, slowly cutting out doorways and then the interior of a proposed church. So the roof of a church is at ground level, the rest of the monument is below ground level, there is no sign of these buildings when looking towards the site, from the distance. However in recent years the Ethiopian and later UNESCO placed protective roofing over some of them, as exposure to the elements of the soft stone that they are carved from, has led to serious deterioration, in some cases.

Almost no light enters into the interior of the various churches, and yet the interiors are very well finished, some with detailed carvings or painted walls. As Peter Garlake comments,

> Even if the spaces were only roughed out in the first stages of excavation, the final space was implicit in almost every part of its detail. As one cut out the apex of a dome, for instance, one had to have a precise sense of its final diameter, of the span of its pendentives, of bay sizes, of column and arch dimensions, and capital and column forms. The churches are not only testimonies to masonry skills; they are even more monuments to their architects' powers of logical thought, foresight, imagination, and ability to be in charge of every aspect of the {complex} work. (3)

So these are magnificent world-class achievements, a sign of just how sacred to king Lalibela was the task of building them. As we explore the different monuments, we shall see that they have a consistent mystical theme, which makes sense of the apparently jumbled maze of buildings and tunnels. Tunnels run discreetly underground, some connecting one church or sanctuary to another, others going apparently nowhere; some are burial places, with small numbers of skeletons lying in them.

Two of the monuments pre-date the time of Lalibela by centuries, and are possibly non-Christian in origin. One monument has a kind of sunken concourse in which there are very deep wells and deep below the ground, a subterranean hall, full of columns, flooded with water.

The geographical context of the southern part of the complex is clear from our diagram. The monuments are wrapped around two small hills, off to one side of the road to Lalibela, but of course all the buildings are underground, and surrounded by a deep trench.

In the centre is the so-called Hill of Golgotha also called the hill of bread, with its winding path surmounted by a strange circular chamber. One gets the impression very soon upon investigating that there is indeed a veiled mystical inspiration behind this site, and it is only when this intention is perceived that the over-all site can be appreciated fully.

Illustrations 2 and 3 also show the relative positions and layout of the churches, and the extensive system of tunnels. These colour-coded diagrams clarify the considerable complexity of the multi-level structures of the site. It appears that the priests in earlier centuries accessed these monuments by means of the tunnels. The reason for this is unknown.

The diagrams cannot of course convey the atmosphere that exists around these unusual buildings, excavated as they were out of the ground, linked by dark tunnels and sited within deep trenches. But the immediate impression is that the idea behind the effort to implement such unique architecture and to link the buildings in this mysterious way, comes from a spiritual or transcendent experience. And the sheer remoteness of the site reinforces on the visitor, the sacred, other-worldly quality of Lalibela.

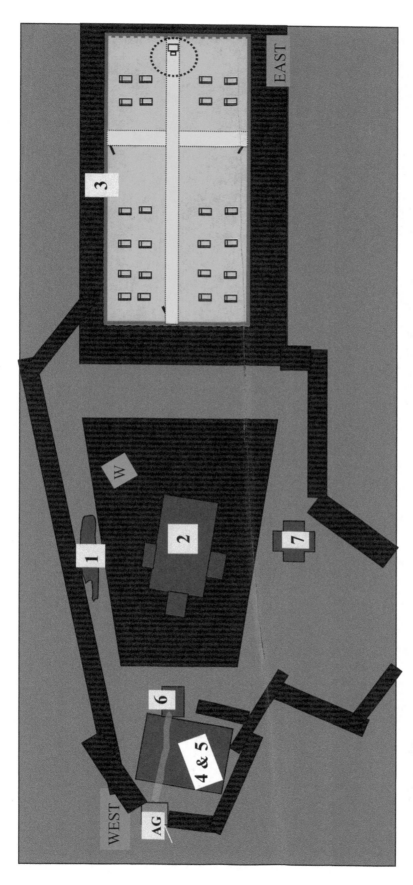

2   Lalibela North side: 1; Maskal , **2**: Maryam, **3**; Medhanie Alem **4 & 5** : Golgotha-Mikael, **6**; Trinity crypt, **7**: Sanctuary of Virgins AG; Adam's Grave (linked by tunnel to #6 , W: a water cistern

13

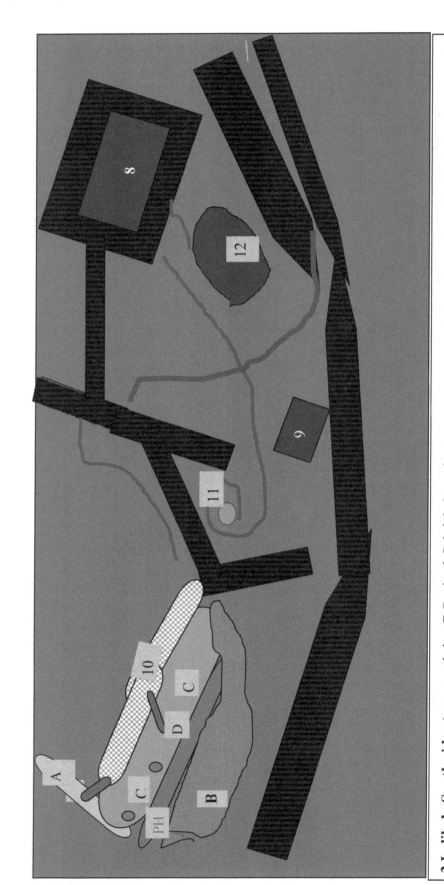

3 Lalibela South side: A :narrow ledge, **B**:Raphael-Gabriel, **C**: ancient pagan water course, **D**: Doors on high wall, **PH**: Path to Heaven with 7 doors, **8**: Emmanuel, **9**: Abba Lianos, **10**: a galley-like passage, **11**: Hill of Bread, **12**: Mercurios. Tunnels shown in brown or green

The Church of St. George.

One of the monuments, the Church of St. George (Guiorgius), is a very fine building, and the most often photographed, because it is viewed as representative of Lalibela in general. It is certainly worthwhile noting this building as a precursor to the actual site because it shows the architectural nature of the monuments. The website 'www.Selamta.net' gives a good overview:

> The monolithic Bet Giorgis, dedicated to the national saint of Ethiopia is isolated from the other two groups of churches. It is located in the southwest of the village on a sloping rock terrace. In its deep pit with perpendicular walls it can only be reached through a tunnel that is entered from some distance away through a trench. Small round caves and chambers have been found in the walls of the courtyard graves for pious pilgrims and monks. The church is described as Lalibela's most elegant and refined in its architecture and stonemasonry. Although its floor plan is of a cross with nearly equal arms, the church is properly orientated, the main entrance being in the west, the holy of holies in the east.
>
> The roof decoration, often represented as the symbol of the Lalibela monuments on photographs and postcards, is a relief of three equilateral Greek crosses inside each other. On the north, south and west sides, gutters and spouts drain the water from the roof.

The famous fashion designer, Calvin Klein, who is obviously very sensitive to the form and style of all objects, visited here, and said about this church,

> Lalibela is just an astonishing place. It's hard to fathom the amount of physical labour that went into chipping this church out of solid granite with nothing but hand tools. And the aesthetic is staggering: a blend of austerity and intricacy, hard angles and soft curves,

that make it feel both deeply ancient and extremely modern all at once". (4)

In addition to the architectural elements, there are also symbolic measurements incorporated into the design of these monuments. One becomes aware that the church of St. George actually has a deliberate numerical symbolism embedded into it. For example, the number 3 and also 3 x 3, as well as the number 12 are incorporated into it. This church is 12 metres high (or rather, deep), and almost 12 m long x 12 m broad (12.9m x 12.5m); and has 12 windows carved into the upper section. It has 3 monumental doors each with 3 x 3 frames; it has 3 shallow steps, 3 steep steps and 3 side steps leading to the main entrance.

It is very likely that the number 12 here refers to the 12 tribes of Israel or the 12 Disciples of Christ. And the 3 x 3 motif probably refers to the nine ranks of divine hierarchies or spiritual beings of early mystical Christian literature. These are the Angels, the Archangels, the Principalities, and so on, up to the Seraphim. However, this church is on the edge of the sacred landscape design, in the southwest corner of the area, see illustration 4.

Apart from Bet Giorgis, there are 12 churches at this site, however two of these were not built by Lalibela, so there are really ten monuments in the sacred landscape. But of the ten that he built, one is a single 'twin-church', and another is really a crypt; the holy Trinity Crypt (or Selassie crypt). The crypt is out of bounds to all tourists. It is the most private part of the complex because of its sacred nature.

4 **Biet Giorgius** The church dedicated St. George, showing the remarkable architectural style.

The two other monuments (referred to now as churches) were in existence before king Lalibela's lifetime. Before we explore the features of the site we need to consider how it all originated, namely the spiritual experience which Lalibela underwent.

Who was king Lalibela ?
In the entry for King Lalibela, the Dictionary of Ethiopian Biography tells us that,

> Lalibela was the most outstanding member of the Zagwe dynasty which ruled Ethiopia in the 1100s and 1200s. He was born in Roha, and his father of uncertain name was a nobleman or possibly even king. His half-brother Harbay was ruler, and Lalibela decided to become a hermit in the Tigre mountains to escape his persecutions. Lalibela is also said to have made the difficult pilgrimage to Jerusalem, then in the hands of the Crusaders. Harbay on the other hand tried to have contacts with the Pope in Rome. On his return to Ethiopia, Lalibela made a successful "march on Roha".
>
> Tradition holds that Harbay abdicated in favour of his half-brother. It seems likely that Lalibela had the support of the Ethiopian clergy, who were doubtless opposed to a Papal alliance. On ascending the throne in 1181 or 1182 Lalibela took the throne name of Gebre Meskel.... It is said that King Lalibela fell ill at the age of 70 and died on 22 June 1220. According to some sources an Egyptian Christian refugee by name Sidi Mesqel was the principal architect and engineer of the rock churches. This was possibly in the early 1200s. It is claimed that Sidi Mesqel was buried in the Medhane Alem church. (5)

So what kind of spiritual experience was it that led Lalibela to construct this unique site? Does it have any links to the well-known three day religious ritual of the Hellenistic Mysteries?

As we explore its artwork and the over-all architectural landscape, it becomes clear that a specific spiritual message is incorporated in the design features of Lalibela. And these features are best understood when they are compared with mystical artwork or texts from ancient Egypt or from medieval Europe! Also the experience that Lalibela underwent, as recorded in the stories of his life, are best understood when it is considered in the light of what we know about the ancient Grecian Mysteries.

In exploring Lalibela, one is actually trying to get inside the original 13th mystical inspiration that led to the construction of these monuments. This is not an easy task, as very little written works were left behind by Lalibela, and reference today to these mystical ideas by the Ethiopian church is rare. And complicating matters, the clergy of the Lasta Highlands apparently did not develop communications with the clergy in the rest of the country. This is indicated in a report from the 1930's by a Swedish Christian nurse who wrote about her time in Lalibela (see below). After Lalibela's death, the site soon became assimilated into the normal beliefs and practises of Ethiopian Christians. Furthermore, over the centuries the volcanic rock has suffered from water erosion and general exposure to the elements, so the more intriguing artwork is now hard to really see clearly, in places.

Chapter Two: the mystical experience behind the site

Rare information about Lalibela's 3-day sleep

There are several semi-historical, semi-legendary accounts of the life of king Lalibela found in Ethiopian religious writings. These vary in their details, but they all present an account of his life which shows that he underwent a spiritual experience. He fell into a kind of sleep that lasted three days, but in fact he is described having an out-of-body experience during this time, not just a sleep. It was an experience in which the king had a vision of the site that he was to build, with its unusual layout and unusual churches. When the reports of his experience are looked at more closely, it becomes apparent that king Lalibela underwent a spiritual experience similar to the three-day initiatory process of the ancient Mysteries. The records tell of how after being poisoned, he entered a death-like sleep state which lasted three-days.

The three-day sleep outcome was perhaps triggered off accidentally; causing an equivalent outcome to the special procedure that induced the initiatory experience in the Mysteries. This is the so-called katabasis experience of the ancient Greek Mysteries, a procedure that also lasted for three days, during which the acolyte descended in their soul into the Netherworld. Throughout the Mystery Religions of the Hellenistic world, it is believed that in this three-day period the acolyte left the physical world and entered into the spirit world, to experience their deity or other spiritual realities.

As we shall see, this was how Lalibela's experience was interpreted in Ethiopia, too. It seems very likely that he actually underwent a specific mystical process, and that later in these semi-legendary church records of his life, this experience was rationalised into the story about an attempt to poison him. There are two primary versions of his life story, written about 500 years ago in Ge'ez, an Ethiopian language and in Amharic, the official language of Ethiopia. Both legends are officially regarded as semi-legendary. One is known by the Ethiopian name, the Gaderla or Gerla Lalibela

20

(the life of Lalibela), the other version is the French version because it is primarily known in the West through a French translation.

This other version of his life story is recorded on a late medieval manuscript, now kept in the British Museum. This document was translated by a French scholar, Prof. Perruchon, and given the title, La Vie de Lalibala (i.e., The Life of Lalibela). Both are late medieval books (made of parchment), copies of which are kept in various churches in Ethiopia, including in Lalibela itself. (6,7) In the French version is said that it is God who directed Lalibela, during his out-of-body experience, to build the churches. Whereas in the Gaderla, (in German and Portuguese versions) it is said to be an Angel who directs him to do this, and that Angels helped in the building of these monuments.

A complete translation of the Gaderla has never been made, but extracts of it are known in translation. A Jesuit priest, Pedro Paez who visited about 1600 AD recorded some of material from the Gaderla, as did Father Francisco Alvares in 1520 AD in his report on the enigmatic Prester John, a mythical ruler from somewhere in the East, who became the focus of attention of the Roman Church, in their search for powerful allies in the Middle East and northern Africa. In the 1930's a Swedish missionary nurse, Anna Lena Röstin acquired extracts of the French version, in an Ethiopian historical book written in Amharic (the Wazema written by Blattengeta Heruy), which she was able to read. I was fortunate to obtain a copy of her book.

When she travelled to Lalibela, the Memhir read to her from the other version, the Gadl, with its own fascinating account of the life of King Lalibela. However, Anna-Lena Röstin had taken with her on this trip the other text with its different version of the legend. Yet, as she notes, the Memhir Heruy had never seen this other version. The differences became a point of interest to both of them, and she reports that these differences between the two accounts were discussed. The

Wazema version mentions persecuted Copts from Egypt helping build the 10 churches; but the Lalibela high priest had not ever heard this before, and insisted that the true story refers to Angels. Ms. Röstin suggested in her prosaic way, that the Ge'ez word understood as 'angels' in the Gerla version, can also be translated "messengers" (just like the Greek word), and hence might really mean the Copts. But, she reports that "the head priest was very reluctant to accept this interpretation." (8)

A few decades later, in the 1950's, a German traveller, H. Pfeiffer, also exploring the life and work of Lalibela, was able to have extracts from this large Ge'ez book, the *Gaderla*, read out to him, by the Memhir at Lalibela. He recorded the more intriguing, mystical points from this document, in German. And also the German scholar, Georg Gerster, also comments on the Gerla in his excellent book, *Churches in Rock*. Gerster undertook extensive exploration of ancient Ethiopian churches in the mid 1960's. He provides invaluable material about the theology and artistic motifs of Ethiopia art in general. However Gerster's perspective, like that of other academic researchers, is naturally not focused on evidence of a mystical message in either the legendary life of king Lalibela, or in the design of his churches.

The story in either version is part of the material accumulated in Ethiopia about the lives of all their saints, and was written about 250 years after Lalibela's death which occurred in the 13th century. Both accounts of his life mention the poisoning incident, and also that it was caused by a family member of Lalibela, (either his brother or step-sister) who wanted to get rid of him, in order to seize his throne. Both accounts mention that Lalibela was placed in a sarcophagus-like niche whilst he lay in a type of coma, and that during this time his soul rose up out of the body and entered into the spirit realms.

One can of course view this period of three-days as just a coincidence, but in any case King Lalibela was in the equivalent of the sarcophagus used for mystical experiences for the same amount of time as occurs in the classical journey into spirit realms by ancient Greek heroes. But was this only by chance, or are there other features to his life's story that confirm a mystical process? Further details in the two accounts of the life of the saint affirm that Lalibela underwent a kind of mystical process. Both versions have really significant points in them, which indicate that a mystical process was involved. But unfortunately knowledge of this is very hard to access. Most reports about Lalibela in books or on the Internet, just say, "As the legend says...." and proceed to give a brief summary in which the most spiritually significant features of his life are omitted.

But here we can look at some actual extracts of the version kept in the British Museum, in the French translation made by P. Perruchon, *La Vie de Lalibala*. We translate from the account, after the episode where Lalibela has been poisoned and laid in the niche in the rock wall, severely affected by the poison. The following account is found at this point...

> God sent one of his radiant angels from amongst his hosts to visit him (Lalibela) and to bring his soul up into heaven to show him the high mysteries...Lalibela became aware of this angel the moment that he drank the poisoned beverage and {so} he raised his soul up to heaven with great joy. (trans. by the author)

The text goes on to describe that Lalibela was raised up to the first, second and third heavens, and beyond these, to all seven heavens. But only brief comments are made about these realms. We have noted in regard to earlier mystery sites that the initiatory process involved the acolyte leaving the body, (which lay quietly in the sarcophagus) over a three-day period whilst the acolyte descended into the Underworld, and later on arose into higher realms. In the Ethiopian accounts, little is said about the Underworld sojourn, but more is said about the higher part of the experience. It is very significant how in the old Ethiopian text the return of Lalibela after three days is described:

Then God ordered the radiant angel to bring Lalibela back onto the Earth and to have his soul re-enter his body. These events {of visiting the many heavens} occurred during the time-period of three-days, during which Lalibela saw the mysteries of the seven heavens, the glory of the angelic beings who dwell therein and….. On the third day he took possession {again} of his body, led by the radiant angel {down to the earth} who carried out the order which God had given him, to bring the soul back into the body from which he had drawn it.[i]   (trans. by the author)

This wording is very intriguing! It doesn't sound like someone recovering from a poison-induced state, or the descriptions of confused ecstasy; it's much more like the classical process of specifically leaving the body for three-days, as reported to occur in the Mysteries. And it is precisely this which is suggested by the narrator of the story, who compares the experience of Lalibela with that of Jonah and of Jesus!

Reports about the three day initiatory sleep: Chronicle One

The Ethiopians themselves understood the experience of Christ on the cross as a katabasis, that is, a descent into the lower soul world or Netherworld. The descent of Jesus into the Netherworld is well known in older theological writings, it figured very largely in very early theological discussion, and was known as the Harrowing of Hades. That the Ethiopians saw the experience in these terms is confirmed by a passage some pages earlier in this same document where we are told that "Christ stayed for three-days and three nights within the entrails of the Earth, he was brought back to life from amidst death..." This statement refers to the ancient legend that says, that whilst Jesus' body was on the cross, he left the cross, in his soul, and descended into Hades, to help the souls of the dead.

The incident involving Jonah is found in the Bible, in the Book of Jonah, and it tells of how an enormous fish swallows up Jonah when he is cast overboard from a boat. After three-days, he is eventually spat back up onto the shore. Jonah speaks of his feelings during his experience, and there are some strange references carefully intermingled with more usual imagery, which indicate that this experience is a three-day initiatory experience, written up in an innocuous manner, for the wider community,

> ...From the depths of Sheol, I called for help, and you listened to my cry.
> You hurled me into the deep, into the very heart of the seas, and the currents swirled about me; all your waves and breakers swept over me...in the troughs of mountains I was sinking into a realm whose bars would hold me forever. But you brought my life up from the pit, O Lord my God. (Book of Jonah 2:2-6)

So here, Jonah actually identifies his location as the Underworld, the realm of the Dead! For the term 'Sheol' is the Hebrew name for the realm of the Dead. It is not the term for the interior of a whale. This incident gives one the impression that Jonah found himself in the foundations or substratum of the earth, on a spiritual level. This is especially obvious when you know that the ancient Hebrews and Greeks and others, believed that the after-life realms (the lower ones) were inside the Earth, and moreover, the really evil realms were located below these, forming the deepest foundations of the Earth's interior.

In this deepest part of the Underworld were the really evil souls and demons, which were held in a kind of barred prison. The mystical writings from the Hellenistic Age (both Greek and Hebrew) report about this sinister realm that if anyone drew near to it, they would feel as if they were in "a realm whose bars would hold me forever." There was a common belief in the Hellenistic world, that the very interior of the

Earth was a kind of barred prison where evil beings were kept; they had been cast down there by the good gods.

The French account of Lalibela's life continues, and sees the experience that Lalibela had, as a kind of Jonah or Jesus experience,

> Lalibela was like the Lord {Jesus} who was brought back to life on the third day, from amidst death. And so he was not like Jonah, who stayed there for three-days and three nights in the belly of the whale, complaining and weeping bitterly. For Lalibela was encompassed in a great joy within the celestial court of the guardian angels...
> (trans. by the author)

So in this Ethiopian document the katabasis experience, or leaving the physical body and making a descent in the soul, is being affirmed as something which not only Lalibela, but also Jesus experienced whilst his body was on the cross, and which Jonah also underwent. So, within the pious religious context of such a public document as this, a hint is carefully given that Lalibela like Jonah was in spirit realms. But we note here that the Ethiopian writer saw a difference between the experience of Jonah and that of Lalibela. Jonah was not given access to the higher divine realms in his katabasis, his experience was restricted to the lower murky realms, but the narrator of the story here is proud to say that, as compared with Jonah, Lalibela's experience was not a murky miserable descent, but one in which the focus was upon the ascent up into higher realms.

Reports about the three day initiatory sleep: Chronicle Two

Now if we look at the other version of the life of king Lalibela, the Gadl or Gerla Lalibela, briefly recorded in German, a similar story unfolds. But here another really important mystical feature is given after Lalibela arises from his sleep and returns to life in this world. The Gerla says that, after awakening out of his sleep, Lalibela rode off on his horse, and began a 40 year journey to special places far away, and eventually reached Jerusalem. The stipulation of a 40 year period is unlikely to be meant literally, but is like the 40 year phases in the life of Moses; it symbolizes the length of time needed to complete a significant phase of the inner spiritual journey. In the German notes of the story in The Gerla Lalibela, it is stated that, after his awoke from his katabasis,

> Lalibela wandered through the wide world for forty years, whilst his wife Makal-Gebra remained behind in Aksum. Lalibela went into Egypt, and there he came to the town of Heliopolis. From there his faithful horse took him to Greece, to the Acropolis, to the land where wise men lived, who called themselves Pythagoreans. And later as he journeyed, he sat at the feet of wise men in a land, whose ruler was once called Zarathustra. And finally he came to Jerusalem. Here he went from holy site to holy site. Here in this land he spoke with many holy men from foreign lands. Finally he underwent baptism in the river Jordan.

The Gadl story from here as noted by Paez and Alvarez goes on to tell how an angel then appeared and proclaimed to him that he was to build the churches. The legend then relates how Lalibela's brother is persuaded to renounce the throne. In the vision he is commanded to do this, to go and meet Lalibela as he returns from Jerusalem, and to formally hand over rulership of Ethiopia to him. Lalibela returned to Ethiopia, became the ruler, and started building the special site, based on an initiatory Christianity, at the place then called Roha, but now named Lalibela after him.

He adopted the additional names of Gebre Maskal; Gebre means Gabriel (the archangel who appeared to him in a vision) and Maskal means the cross (the symbol of Christ). After the site was completed, Lalibela renounced his throne and taught people for three years in the churches, until his death. It is reported that during this time of helping his people, one day whilst he was teaching and contemplating, Christ Jesus appeared to him.

It appears that the life of Lalibela is partly historical and partly a veiled presentation of a mystical process. But the German notes of the Gaderla also indicate the kind of heretical Christianity to which Lalibela felt affinity, a version of Christianity wherein Christ is viewed as somehow linked to the sun god who was revered in various ancient religions.

For as we saw above the Gaderla says that riding on his faithful horse, Lalibela's journeying took him to the sacred Egyptian town of Heliopolis and that he then went to Greece, to Athens, to the land of the Acropolis, where he encountered some students of the Greek sage, Pythagoras. Then he journeyed on to the land of the Magi, meeting wise men who were students of the Persian sage, Zarathustra, and then finally he journeyed on to Jerusalem.

We note at this point firstly that in the 13th century there were no longer any Pythagoreans in Greece, as they had died out a few centuries after Pythagoras; so about 200 BC. Although a few loosely defined neo-Pythagorean existed up to the fourth century AD, this is still 800 years before Lalibela. So how do we relate to these apparently pagan beliefs which venerated the sun god, in the account of the life of Lalibela? Basically, although the stories are semi-legendary, they are very significant to understanding the site.

For although this life of Lalibela is part of Ethiopian religious literature, the reports actually contain some striking references to mystical processes. So, whilst they cannot be taken as historically precise in all details, there are a number of esoteric statements that are very significant, giving these texts a substantial authority.

They have authority with regard to what really mattered to Lalibela, namely the mystical side of Christianity, not only the historical details of how long a king reigned, and who succeeded him, and when, etc. We conclude that this was also what really mattered to those who succeeded him, the clergy whose task it evidently was to guard the deeper perspective of their religion.

Christ and the Egyptian sun god

In fact the association of Christ with the sun god is not unique to Lalibela. For throughout Ethiopia, Christ is depicted in artistic decorations found inside churches as the sun, or he is referred to as solar in various manuscripts. As Gerster reports from his extensive search for religious sites in Ethiopia, the image of the sun is usually encountered in Ethiopian churches directly above the main entrance or the sanctuary arch, or both places.

Such a tradition can be seen as a purely poetic metaphor, with no pagan implications at all. For example, we find the reference to the Messiah as the sun, in Isaiah and in the late prophet, Malachi. In these books, the Messiah is referred to metaphorically as a solar deity. But in Ethiopia this attitude to Christ became a very prominent motif, with depictions of Christ as the sun with a face in it, as if it is more than a symbol.

For example, in the church of Gannata Maryam, and of Makina Madhane Alem, elsewhere in Ethiopia, Christ is depicted within a round solar disc, as a counterpart to the moon, which is also given a face. And in other churches, the sun and the moon are depicted with a face in an ambiguous manner which suggests that the personified sun is also Christ.

Then at Lalibela, Christ appears again as in effect a round solar disc, in the church of Maryam, but as we shall see, other features at Lalibela go much further, indicating that it is not a metaphor or poetic image, but rather it is seen as a reality.

Chapter Three: the heresy of a cosmic saviour

Lalibela and the spiritual sun

The reference to Pythagoras and to Heliopolis is very intriguing; this name means in Greek, the city of the sun. The town of Annu (also called On or Heliopolis) was the sacred site of the sun worship cult in old Egypt, and its priesthood was behind the impetus to build the Great Pyramid. But this town was just an ancient ruin in the 13th century, having been reduced to rubble by the invading Persians about 1,800 years before Lalibela. Heliopolis, which was certainly not a Christian centre in the usual sense, cannot be regarded as a part of the Christian religion.

In the Old Kingdom of Egypt, from about 3000 BC, it was the primary sacred site for the Sun Mysteries of Egypt. Moreover it is reported that Pythagoras had studied at Heliopolis for 22 years. The Pythagoreans, the students of Pythagoras, had long ago ceased to exist, just as Heliopolis was long gone. But like other mythic accounts from esoteric sources, the legendary life of Lalibela is presenting key spiritual themes, not mundane facts. However, the reference to Heliopolis together with Pythagoras brings a very specific type of old mystical wisdom into direct focus, namely the worship of the sun god. How can we as modern people relate to this?

It appears that in the holistic consciousness of earlier eras, the cosmos was experienced as en-souled, so to speak. And the ancients believed that perception of another level of creation, beyond molecular substance, was enhanced by their spiritual processes. At least that was obviously the intention behind the complex initiatory systems instituted in earlier ages. From literature of the Grecian era, and from earlier Babylonian writings, it is clear that the ancients considered the planets to be en-souled, they were not just a physical, molecular object; they had a kind of consciousness or soul. This view went in parallel with their holistic view of the human being, who also had a soul, apart from the body. In these old systems of spirituality, people had, in addition to a soul, a life-force organism, a body of subtle life energies. Each planet and the sun had an indwelling spiritual being, and these were called the planetary Intelligence or the spirit of each planet; by the Greco-Latin era they were given specific names. The spirit of the sun was a much greater divinity than the planetary spirits, just as the sun is physically greater than the planets.

This view that the sun has a great spiritual reality behind its physical form remained a doctrine into the era of Hellenistic Mystery cults and it survived right into the first centuries of the Christian era, through the cult of Mithra. In fact, in 316 AD the new Christian emperor, Julian the Apostate, was initiated into the cult of Mithra, and he wrote a treatise about the triune sun.

He believed that the sun exists firstly, on a high transcendental level, and secondly on a less transcendent, more soul level where it is worshipped as Helios or Mithra and it is this sun that is associated with hosts of angelic beings. And then thirdly, it exists as the visible sun disc. Any such view of the sun was similar to the old Egyptian religion, where the sun disc was regarded as an outer physical form of a sublime spirit being, called Ra or Osiris.

Now what is so intriguing here is that in the early years of Christianity, amongst some adherents of this new religion, there was also an understanding that the 'Christ' was actually the great sun god and that Jesus was a very holy man, who was the vessel of this deity. One example of this attitude is found in the writings of a great early Christian mystic theologian who lived in Egypt, Origenes of Alexandria.

The sun god and old Egyptian Christianity
There is a really striking passage in his Commentary on the Gospel of St. John, where Origenes teaches that there is a cosmic aspect to Christ. He seems to be saying that this name refers to not just one, but two high spirit beings. There is firstly the Logos, who is in the Trinity, and hence near to the uncaused Godhead. And yet secondly there is also another

aspect of Christ; where he is considered to be the highest of a certain rank of high spirits known in the Bible as the Mighty Spirit-hosts,

> ….there are certain beings, {who are} spiritual, divine, living-beings; referred to as Mights (i.e., mighty spirit hosts), of whom Christ was the highest and the finest. So Christ is designated not only the Wisdom of God (the sublime Logos), but {also} the Might of God. (trans. by author)   (9)

Here we have a truly striking statement from a revered and learned Egyptian church father, of a belief which today would be seen as very heretical. He is saying that Christ is a name for two transcendent spirit beings, namely the highest of the Mighty Spirit-hosts and also the Logos. The Logos is a particularly high being, similar to what was known as the World-Soul to Hellenistic mystics. And therefore by implication to these Christians, Jesus is a man; a man who became the vessel of these divine being(s). To know more about this passage from Origenes, and the ancient Christian sun-god idea, see my ebook, The Grecian Mysteries & Christianity.

A further example of this belief is found in Origenes' commentary on the Gospel of St. John. There Origenes says that Christ illuminates the souls of human beings, as though they were illumined by the sun (just as the physical sun illumines the body), and that this enables such spiritualized persons to be able to see other spiritual beings. But he also says that the souls questing for mystical spirituality are in fact absorbing non-physical or spiritual light from the spiritual sun. And for those who don't seek this mystical illumination, the spiritual writings in the Bible are still of great if somewhat lesser value. He puts his astounding holistic perspective like this,

"For those for who "do not take up into themselves the solar rays of the Christ", the apostles and prophets offer some (weaker) illumination".

One could of course simply see this as a poetic image. But in view of other statements from Origenes, which we don't have space to explore here, it appears to be meant literally. This is one reason no doubt for the works of Origenes being banned as heretical some centuries after his death. Now, with regard to Lalibela, it seems as if he had a view of Christianity that was not so different from that of Origenes, and that both men seem to have a view that is similar to the ancient Egyptian sun god religion.

Ethiopia is of course, part of the African continent as is Egypt, and so the possibility exists that Ethiopian Christianity may have at one time been influenced by a stream of early 'solar' Christianity, with its Egyptian qualities. This stream was strongly represented by Origenes, living in the Egyptian port city of Alexandria. This was a religious movement that saw a link between the Ra-Osiris solar religion of Egypt and that of the new religion, Christianity; whose Saviour said, "I am the light of the world".

Ethiopia's St. George as Horus, helper of the sun god

It is quite possible that there may be some theological beliefs in Ethiopian Christianity that are derived from the Egyptian sun god religion. When we explore the wonderful church of Biet Maryam we shall find some evidence of this. And we can also note that in the church of Gannata Maryam there is evidence of Egyptian mystical beliefs about the sun god. In this church there is a depiction of a figure who is slaying a dragon, and it is identified with a famous Christian saint, Hor, the hermit, the dragon-slayer.

But as Gerster comments, the story of the life of this saint does not correlate to the motif of being a dragon slayer! In the drawing inside the church, the person or deity is throttling a serpentine monster, (not a dragon) who is swallowing a ram. Gerster mentions the suggestion from a French scholar in East African studies, A. Caquot, that this seems to portray an incident in the life of the Egyptian god Horus! Such a strange intrusion into Christian Ethiopian beliefs of an ancient Egyptian belief is seen by scholars as being quite possible, through what is called cultural osmosis. Since Ethiopia is part of Africa, and it is known that there were cultural and commercial links between Ethiopia and Egypt, such osmosis is possible. Especially if there was an underlying attitude amongst Ethiopian Christians that their Saviour was a solar deity. In any event, in the Egyptian book of the Dead and elsewhere, Horus as representative of the sun god, destroys the serpent Apep.

Summing up, a key to understanding the features of Lalibela is to realize that these legends of his mystical experience appear to be hinting that, to Lalibela Christ was a deity, a kind of continuation of the Egyptian sun god. The connection of king Lalibela to a solar deity or divine sun spirit is strengthened further through the episode reported in these stories of the life of Lalibela, which associates Lalibela with bees.

Bees were regarded as special creatures in the holistic consciousness of earlier ages, in many cultures. They were regarded as little co-workers of the sun god, with their way of gathering nectar on sunny days and then making the warm golden honey. The legend recounts that when he was a tiny infant, a swarm of bees appeared near Lalibela's cradle, as if summoned by his presence, and in fact his name Lalibela means, "the bees are aware of his sovereignty." To this day, at the church called Bet Emmanuel (no. 8 in our diagrams) there are some cavities in the outer wall of the courtyard that are set aside for sacred bees to live in.

And another association of Lalibela with the sun, in the passage from the above story, is the reference to him visiting Zarathustrian sages in Persia. This great Prophet, who lived about 600 BC, proclaimed and established the veneration of a deity of boundless light, called Ahura Mazdah, who battles against an evil power of darkness. This radiant deity manifests through a number of beings, and these enable it to become active in different ways. Perhaps the most lofty of these beings is Mazdah-Mithra. Mazdah-Mithra is a solar deity, a representative of the sun. A core prayer of the Zarathustrians, when earthly tasks are over was may they, with the help of Mazdah-Mithra, arrive at "…that luminous space, that highest of all things…" It is obviously the sun-sphere that is meant here. (10) So this religion can also be seen as involved in a kind of sun god cult.

So why are these extraordinary travels which hint at the pagan sun god, placed in the life of the devout Christian king, Lalibela? These Ethiopian biographical stories provide a hint that Christ is viewed as the same great central being who was worshipped in the religions of ancient Egypt and Persia. In effect, the legendary accounts of Lalibela's life include a time after his three-day special sleep, in which he was given a special wisdom, associated with the sun. It appears that these legendary accounts of the life of Lalibela are hinting that in some ways he saw Christianity as a new form of the ancient reverence of the sun spirit.

But is this analysis true? Are there any features of this amazing site, which show signs of such an heretical form of Christianity? As we noted, it was during his sleep that, according to the legend, an angel appeared to Lalibela, and gave him a vision of the churches, and the admonition to build them. If this site is explored carefully, but with a sense for religious ideas, a considerable degree of mystical Christianity can be seen underlying the design of this site. There is a definite sacred landscape behind the really complex arrangement of tunnels, sanctuaries, churches and hills. These features, and the incidents about Lalibela's life, such as the three-day sleep, leads one to the conclusion that Lalibela underwent some form of the three-day initiatory process that the Mysteries had used for millennia.

Chapter Four: reading the sacred landscape

The mystical message in the layout of the northern side of the site

The first building in the site proper, No.1 in our diagram, is called Biet Maskal; meaning The Sanctuary of the Cross. It is in effect a broad gallery chapel, which has been carved out of a kind of bulge in the northern wall of the nearby building, Biet Mariam; which is also known as The Church of Virgin Mary. Sanctuary no. 7 is called Biet Danagel, meaning The Sanctuary of the Virgins, and it juts out from the opposite side of the Church of Mary (Biet Mariam), it partly incorporates a grotto, and is in effect a small chapel. Its name may refer to a group of virgins who were martyred long ago, or it may refer to the 10 virgins of the parable of Christ (Matthew 25:1). It is also the case that the divine being or person to whom a church at Lalibela was originally dedicated is not always really known; it varies in reports and in the oral traditions of the site.

In illustration 2, there is a group of features at the western side of the northern section; these include the large monolithic rock, called Adam's Grave and the twin churches of Michael and Golgotha. From a hole in the floor of the Golgotha church, a tunnel leads to the holy sanctum, the Trinity Crypt. This underground tunnel to the private Trinity Crypt (CT) is indicated in grey.

The spiritual journey hidden in the layout and planning of the site in its northern side, takes the mystically-aware pilgrim on a journey through the deeper secrets of a cosmopolitan Christianity. You start by walking along the narrow trench up to Adam's Grave. This block of stone has been hollowed out, making an opening in its lower area. Through it you can proceed on to the sanctuaries, moving from west to east. But once you have passed through the monolith called Adam's Grave, you face a decision, because you come to a Parting of the Ways. This is rather like the passageway inside the Great Pyramid of Egypt where, as you enter the descending corridor, and come to about where the granite plug is located, you can either go downwards or take the path up into the Grand Gallery. The path downwards leads to the stifling dark subterranean chamber that goes nowhere; or you take to the path upwards to the Grand Gallery and eventually arrive at the initiatory chambers.

Adam's Grave

Once you are through Adam's Grave, you can go to the left, and then gradually the narrow trench will broaden out, and although this path is easy, it simply escorts you right away from the rest of the complex, up along a broadening route, until you are alone in a barren, arid landscape. If however, you go to the right, you proceed along a narrow trench pathway and then approach the twin churches Golgotha-Michael which are dedicated to the core Christian theme of Golgotha, the place where Jesus was crucified.

And the theme of Mount Sinai is also a focus. Mount Sinai is traditionally identified as the place where Moses experienced God (Yahweh) appearing in the burning bush. The church has also has been dedicated to another sacred being, to the archangel Michael, who is central in ancient mystical texts and legends from both Jewish and Christian sources. This archangel is mentioned in extra-Biblical Hellenistic documents as the special guide for acolytes in the spiritual quest, as they raise their consciousness up to spirit realms. Now the trench design at Adam's Grave is in fact an embodiment of the New Testament admonition from Jesus to walk the narrow path, not the easy broad path, through which you cannot enter heaven, in Matthew 7:13-14:

> "Enter through the narrow gate. For wide is the gate and broad is the road that leads to destruction, and many enter through it. But small is the gate and narrow the road that leads to life, and only a few find it."

The Golgotha church and the Michael or Debra Sina (Mount Sinai) church

The church known as Debra Sina (Mount Sinai), also dedicated to archangel Michael, is exposed on three sides by the excavated trench, and the northern side leads into Biet Golgotha. This church of Golgotha is accessed by a door from the church of Michael/Debra Sina, which is more like a small annex, rather than a chapel. This church is not so well carved out it is somewhat unfinished inside. However it has more features than the adjacent church of Debra Sina. For it has four life-size carvings of saints. In its northern wall there is a small recess, protected by a grill, referred to as the Tomb of Christ or the Jesus cell. In this small cell there is a recumbent figure of a man, with no features on his face, lying in an arcosolium or specially shaped sarcophagus, and there is an angel standing at his feet. Beatrice Playne reported;

> Golgotha, which opens out of Mikael and whose very existence could easily be missed, is rather crude in comparison and appears to be used more as a vestry and store than as a church. Yet it is here that one finds the four life-size figures of saints, carved in deep relief in the walls of the church. At one time, I am sure that these were painted, as I found traces of turquoise blue and white on their moulded niches.... Because these figures have their feet at ground level, or only slightly raised from it, they give an almost frightening sense of reality. I could find no satisfactory reason for the decay of two of the figures on the opposite wall and am inclined to think that this is due to a change in the nature of the rock itself....I fancy there must be a wedge of softer stone here. It is noteworthy that Alvarez only speaks of two figures so that it looks as if the others had already deteriorated by the sixteenth century.

> As sculptural reliefs, the two remaining figures are exceedingly fine. I do not think that there is anything like them in any of the other ancient churches in

Ethiopia. Although they cannot be considered typical, I think they are nearer to Coptic sculpture than to any other. After all, Egyptian workmen are thought to have been employed in Lalibela. All four were covered with curtains, so that even if one had penetrated as far as this inner church and was ignorant of the existence of these reliefs, one would never see them. (11)

There is another recess in this church which is called the Tomb of Lalibela, suggesting that the saint's body is interred there. Both of these recesses are curtained off. This group of monuments is devoid of any architectural features that would link them to the usual Ethiopian building style, the Axumitic. They are more like other forms of Ethiopian architecture, whereas there are several monuments elsewhere in this site that show the Axumite style quite clearly.

The Crypt of the Trinity or the Selassie Chapel
The Crypt of the Trinity, also known as the Selassie Chapel, is built at the eastern side of the Golgotha church. In addition to access from an underground tunnel starting back at Adam's Grave, there is access from the church of Golgotha via a doorway at the eastern end of the right-hand nave, and this opens onto the Selassie Chapel. Michael Gervers describes it very well, and concludes that it was the last of the ten monuments to be excavated here,

> … The final excavation, and perhaps the last of any of the rock-cut monuments in Lalibäla, was the Sellassie Chapel. It must have followed the completion of {the church of} Golgotha because it can only be entered through the doorway at the east end of Golgotha's south aisle; and it must have followed the excavation of the Jesus cell, as its SW corner is excavated on an angle in order not to cut into and obliterate the cell's east wall. This crypt is accessed through a simple doorway at the east end of Golgotha's south aisle. It is in fact, no more a crypt than any other

rock-cut monument in Lalibäla because it is on the same underground level as the Däbrä Sina and Golgotha churches, and has no vertical link to the surface. It is, however, an exceptionally dark spot, since natural light comes only through a single, small window in the SW corner, and is held to be such a holy place that few people outside the superior ranks of the priesthood have ever been granted access to it. (12)

The crypt is a private holy space for the senior priests at Lalibela. Inside it is fairly bare, having three square stone altars, one of which has the four apocalyptic animals carved into it; eagle, bull, lion and human. Behind these three altars are two carvings on the rear wall, the one on the left has a very strong appearance of being an ox. But shown as upright, with the body of a man, and clad in priestly vestments. The other carving on the right is so badly damaged as to be nearly obliterated; nothing is really visible there now. But it is rumoured by a traveller in the 1960's that a priest eventually told him that it was of an ass (i.e., donkey). (13)

In the Nativity story presented in Luke's Gospel (2:27), it is told how Jesus was born in a manger, and hence he was amongst domestic animals. It became traditional in Christianity that these same two animals were present in the manger when Jesus was born. If it were an ox and an ass, then the mystical-esoteric theme presented here (and in the gospel) probably concerns the contrast between the divine human aspect (Jesus) and two primary strands of the lower qualities in the human being.

Now there are various enigmas at Lalibela in terms of history and architecture, apart from its mystical message. It is very hard to date because the architecture is unique in places, and also because the mixture of architectural styles here is also unique to Ethiopia. For example, this special crypt or chapel, which is rumoured to be the burial site of Lalibela, is considered by one critic as belonging to a time after Lalibela. As we noted above, it has monolithic altars; and such a feature in any Ethiopian church is usually dated to about 1380 at the earliest, or one hundred years after Lalibela. (14)

Another enigma is the carved figures of the apocalyptic creatures, etc, in the crypt, and the larger-than-life carvings of saints in the Golgotha church. The presence of statues or bas-relief carvings of people in a church is unique to all Ethiopia; and indeed some experts conclude that they derive from the 15th century. These carvings may just possibly date from a later period, but nevertheless, the Trinity Crypt itself can be regarded as a feature created by Lalibela himself. As we shall see from a careful consideration of the sacred landscape and the esoteric features in these monuments, one can be certain that it was under instruction from king Lalibela that these ten monuments here were constructed.

But after his lifetime additional features may have been added to what he had created. The design and carvings inside the Selassie Crypt (or Trinity Crypt) derive from the same spiritual perspective that Lalibela has placed in the other monuments. Part of the confusion here is that it is precisely Lalibela's creative technique to mix styles, or indeed to create his own style.

If a remarkable person sets out on the basis of a remarkable experience to create a site for the Christian Mysteries, then its features could well be an original creative idea, and not arise in the historical flow of artistic styles, and not stay within normal cultural guidelines. But it is obvious that Lalibela was also building at a site where some earlier monuments had already been existence for centuries, and he may have altered these to suit his purpose.

His designated successors may have re-interred him in a tomb in the Crypt. The criticism that this room is too plain and humble for such a king, is not so relevant if we take into the account the nature of his life. Lalibela is said to have lived as a simple monk in his later years, so he would not have inclined towards being placed after death in a grand mausoleum.

Journeying from West to East (towards the sun)

The key to understanding Lalibela's monuments comes from knowing that it has a spiritual aim behind its design, which is incorporated into its architecture. Walking on in the trench, beyond the twin church with its crypt, you will find yourself on the pathway to the church called Biet Maryam (Church of Mary). Then, if you keep on going, the path will take you to a church called Medhanie Alem which translates as The Saviour of the World.

This large building is not only a splendid church in its own right, it is also a sanctuary which symbolizes the new Global Community of Goodwill, in the sense of the Christmas message of peace on Earth and goodwill amongst people. Its design appears to embody a special theme from Lalibela's mystical experience about the significance for humanity of the Christ coming to the Earth. But to understand this, we must go back to the start of the journey, where Adam's Grave is located.

A Pillar to Melchizedek and Adam

This feature provides a strong indication that to Lalibela, the Christ was a cosmic being, and Jesus was a separate human being, and the Christ was somehow seen as linked to the great sun spirit of the other earlier solar religions, such as that of Osiris, Ahura Mazdah, and Apollo. The idea that Adam lies buried here (naturally this is understood to be a symbolic statement) refers to a core theme of esoteric Christianity that was contemplated in eastern Christianity, but was not a focus of interest in western churches.

Now, normally it would be quite compatible in a Christian sacred site of either eastern or western origin, to have something representing Adam, because in Christian theology, Christ came to the world to undo the negative circumstances triggered off by Adam and his fall from Paradise. But here we have **the grave** of Adam, as we noted earlier. Why is the grave of Adam placed here? We find the answer in a rare old Syriac Christian text, called The Cave of Treasures, which is a religious text that has long been revered in Ethiopia. This scripture says that when the great Flood came over the Earth, Adam's body was placed on Noah's Ark, and then, when the waters finally subsided he was buried near Jerusalem, with the help of the mysterious being called Melchizedek. (15) So who is Melchizedek? Melchizedek is mentioned early in the Bible, in Genesis 14:27. He is a very holy, but very mysterious being who actually bestowed upon Abraham his mission of founding the Hebrew nation. So the implication is that he is spiritually actually a higher being than Abraham. This is a situation that has caused a lot of questions amongst theologians over the centuries.

One explanation for bringing in this reference to Melchizedek is to reinforce the underlying concept that this site here at Roha (later called Lalibela) was to become a kind of alternative Jerusalem. And this is certainly true, because king Lalibela was inspired to create a kind of copy of Jerusalem. An alternative to Jerusalem was needed in the 13th century, because the Muslims had triumphed over the crusaders in the battle for the Holy Lands; so access to Jerusalem for pilgrims was now all but gone. It is reported in the mystical Cave of Treasures that Adam was buried at Golgotha by Melchizedek. So, this means that the new site in Ethiopia, as a kind of alternative to the actual Golgotha, must also have its own Grave of Adam. And for this reason also, the name of the nearest church to this large stone is called the Church of Golgotha.

But it is also the case that in early mystical Gnostic Christian circles, Melchizedek was regarded not as a person, but as a high spiritual being; a being who is described as having the task of helping the spiritual light, which radiates out from the spiritual sun (they thought of it as perhaps a spiritual version of sunlight), to reach the Earth in a purified form. In such mystical texts, the cosmic aspect of Christ is viewed as a form of the sun spirit, and Jesus is seen as a human vessel of this being. Such an other-worldly, transcendent idea is of course very alien to western theology, but it was not so in the first centuries of Christianity in Egypt, Syria and Ethiopia.

So, if Adam's Grave is placed right at the beginning of the sacred journey at Lalibela, is this hinting that the pilgrim who was to make the long and arduous journey here, in the foothills of the Lasta mountains, should meditate upon the idea that this deeply revered being, Melchizedek, has somehow been here or blessed this site? It is very likely that this is exactly the case, because it was Melchizedek who gave to Abraham his mission of becoming the founder of the Israelites. And Ethiopian Christianity has always been very Hebraic in its flavour. For example, every church has key Old Testament symbols in it, such as a small, simple wooden object representing the Ark of the Covenant.

This more mystical perspective, which is natural to the ancient Ethiopian church, considered the idea of angels and spiritual beings being actively involved in helping humanity quite compatible with their theology. For example in a monastery on Lake Tana, in northern Ethiopia, is a document which mentions costly presents being given to a church by a notable person. The name of this person, which is probably an official title, actually means the Angel of the Sun. (16) This indicates again the more cosmic nature of Ethiopian Christianity. One gains the impression that in medieval Ethiopia one is in a more transcendent, other-worldly form of the Christian religion, than in the West.

The more you are acquainted with the message of the Christian scriptures, their deeper mystical messages, especially through contemplation of them, the more enriching will be a trip to Lalibela. (The Gospel of St. John, with its cosmic focus, and the Gospel of Thomas are useful contemplative texts to use here.) So with all this in mind, one walks on in the trenches excavated from the volcanic rock, and those who have knowledge of Christianity will recall that Jesus is called the second Adam. Adam is in this sense, the first as yet unrefined primal human being, whereas Jesus is the perfected, spiritualized human being; so we have the initial human being and the final, perfected person. Then, walking on to the twin sanctuaries of Golgotha and Archangel Michael, these themes would occupy your mind.

But, if one were permitted to enter the Crypt of the Trinity (and very few people ever are), there one would contemplate the four apocalyptic creatures, carved into the three altars. These four creatures or symbols consist of a bull, lion, eagle and a prototype of the human being. These four creatures appear to represent the primary strands of consciousness on earth, and they are also mentioned in Jewish religious writings. But they are in effect another version of the famous sphinx symbol of ancient Mesopotamia. For the classical sphinx consists of bull, lion, eagle and a prototype of the human being.

These four represent a primary theme in ancient spirituality, namely the triumph of the human mind over the animal tendencies. It appears that to the ancients, these three animal species, the feline (lion), bird (eagle) and ruminant (bull) represent the most fundamental and primordial strands of animal life and thus consciousness. They are like the three bases from which all the other animals have derived. The great drama of humanity's long history, when seen spiritually and ethically, has centred on the struggle to rise above these animal energies, to find a higher, truly human nature. It was exactly this ethical spiritual challenge, especially the mystical esoteric side of it, namely rising up to initiatory consciousness, which was the focus of ancient priesthoods.

So, the acolyte in the secret Selassie Crypt has much to think about for it appears the message from Lalibela here is that the advent of a kind of cosmic Christ signifies great help in overcoming the animalistic nature. Then one leaves this crypt and, walking on, comes to the church of Mary. We shall explore this remarkable initiatory monument in the next chapter, see illustration 5.

5 Biet Maryam   A view of the church of the Virgin Mary. In effect, this monument with its symbolic 'pronaos' (vestibule) is a tabernacle-shaped church designed as a sanctuary for the Divine Feminine.

Chapter Five: the Sanctuary of the Virgin Mary as Isis

The Church of Mary (Biet Maryam)

On the journey eastwards through the site, one is walking in the direction of the sun, which was apparently understood by Lalibela as the symbol of Christ in his solar aspect. We now encounter the most fascinating feature in Lalibela, the remarkable Biet Maryam, or the church of Mary. What is significant here is that this sanctuary is not really formed in the shape of a church; it is more like a house or indeed the tabernacle of the Old Testament. It is basically a rectangular solid building, complete with three covered entrances or porches. But before we step inside, it is really important to note just what is on the outside; some highly mystical relief carvings are to be seen here. And, cut into the eastern wall of this sanctuary are some openings that serve as windows, allowing in some much needed light. We will briefly explore these windows first.

The Templars' cross or a uniquely Ethiopian cross ?

One of these openings is in the form of a cross that has been sensationally described as the cross of the Knights Templar. However the cross is actually of the type known as a 'cross pattée', which was used by various church orders; it was used quite widely in medieval times. One religious Order that was given dispensation by the Pope to use it was the Teutonic Knights; and another Order was the Knights Templar. So, the presence of this window shape at Lalibela does not constitute proof that the Knights Templar were here. There is no evidence of members of the order of Knights Templar ever being in Lalibela; for a discussion of this theme, see the Appendix for more about the Ethiopian cross.

The situation is that this type of cross is of unknown origin, but it goes back to long before the Knights Templar order was created. Crosses of a similar shape also existed in pre-Christian times. But in terms of the Christian religion, the cross pattée could be called the 'Ethiopian cross', because coins with this cross stamped on them were issued as long ago as 350 AD, by the Ethiopian ruler, Emperor Ezana, see illustration 6A. Only a few other crosses similar to this from such an early period in the history of Christendom have been discovered elsewhere, (e.g., at Beth Shan in Israel, and these may not be of Christian origin). The church in Rome adopted it in 780 AD or so; about that time it was bestowed upon Charlemagne. The Knights Templar adopted this cross in 1197, some 850 years later, as did other Orders.[ii] So to call it a Templar cross would be to misrepresent the situation at Lalibela. This type of window indicates the use of a standard Ethiopian cross as an artistic embellishment. One of these Ethiopian crosses is to be found on the ceiling of Biet Maryam, see illustration 6B.

The gammadion cross

Another type of opening cut into the walls is a window in which there is a somewhat rigid version of the famous and misunderstood swastika symbol. After its abuse by the terrifying Hitler regime, this cross is best referred to these days by an older neutral term, such as the gammadion cross. But of course the cross at Lalibela has nothing to do with 20th century fascism. It is intriguing to find this symbol used at Lalibela. The Ethiopian authorities regard this type of cross as originating in Ethiopia, and that it was created by simply altering the traditional Greek cross.

The Greek cross has all four arms of equal length, but the arms are straight. However, in view of the cosmopolitan features here in this remarkable site, it is perhaps just possible that it might derive from the same kind of belief in subtle life energies in the environment, as many other cultures had. It is important to know that this gammadion cross window is also present in at least one other church in Ethiopia, namely St. Michael's church of Dabra Salam. This suggests that this cross is indeed simply an altered version of the traditional Greek cross.

6B Inside BIET MARYAM A partial view of the ceiling . Note the 'cross pattée' on the ceiling, inside the Star of David

6A **Ethiopian 'cross pattée';** placed on a coin from ca.300-350 AD under King Ezana. Not imported by the Knights Templar, but indigenous to Ethiopia, nearly 1,000 years before Lalibela.

The western façade of Biet Maryam: the Egyptian sun god Akeru?

In addition to the cross gammadion and the cross pattée, there are other deeply mystical symbols on the walls of Biet Maryam. On the west wall of this amazing church, at the entrance to the porch, images of two lions have been carved in bas-relief; these are now badly deteriorated. This is an unusual artistic motif for a church dedicated to the Virgin Mary! It is very significant as we noted above that this entrance is not an entrance into the actual church, it goes into a small vestibule or porch.

Now it is known that in non-Christian art, lions in pairs each with the same posture, can be placed as sentinels guarding a valuable site, signifying that something sacred is inside. (A single lion can be a symbol of malignant spirit beings and the corresponding qualities in the human soul). In either role they are certainly not relevant to the Virgin Mary.

However two lions on either side of an entrance to a monument which is associated with some kind of solar Christianity reminds one of an ancient Egyptian symbol. This symbol is found on the Giza plateau, where the sun god Ra has his earthly symbol, the great leonine sphinx, whom the Egyptians called Ra-Harmachis.

Between the paws of the sphinx there is a large stone stele, which was erected by pharaoh Thutmosis IV. Looking at this stele, we can notice that an intriguing scene is carved on it, for it does not have just a solitary sphinx. Instead there are two images of the sphinx, but they are in the posture of two lions, above whom is the winged sun disk. These lions are called the Akeru, and they symbolize the influence of the sun god at sunrise and sunset. This means that on this stele at the Giza plateau, the sphinx as a direct sun symbol **has been merged with the symbol of Akeru**, creating the two lions near a sun disc; these are the earthly manifestation of the sun god, see illustration 7B.

So, these striking images on the sphinx stele represent the Akeru or two lions as helpers of the sun god, but now portrayed as two sphinxes. And the sphinx form itself is a symbol of the sun god. So, on the Giza plateau where the great sphinx faces the rising sun, and behind whom the setting sun descends in the summer, the pharaoh Thutmosis IV placed two carvings of this remarkable being, a combined sphinx-Akeru entity.

This symbol of two lions, especially when placed on either side of the sun-disc, is a symbol in Egypt of Aker (or Akeru); Aker is a dual symbol of the Egyptian sun god, Ra or Osiris, but especially of the rising and the setting sun. Now, this is what seems to be here at Lalibela, for these lions are not shown serenely resting, facing the observer, in the posture as the two lions of classical art.

They have different postures; on the left, the lion is sinking down, and on the right, the lion is rising up. It appears that they are alluding to the setting and the rising sun, as symbolized by the Akeru. And the Akeru represent the setting sun and the rising sun, or **in other words, the sun as experienced on the Earth**. These two lions in ancient Egypt were in effect mediators of the sun god in his activity upon the Earth.

The cosmology taught at the ancient Egyptian town of Heliopolis involved this double lion deity, Akeru. Now, earlier we saw in the legend of his life that Lalibela is said to have gone on a journey to the sacred city Heliopolis. A tantalizing mystical statement, especially since Heliopolis had ceased to exist about 2,000 years earlier.

There was an enclosure of the temple of the sun god in Heliopolis where sacred lions were kept. So what are symbols of the sun god, of his activity upon the Earth, doing in a Christian site, and in particular, at the entrance to a small building which itself is a vestibule leading into the church of St. Mary? See illustration7A.

It is significant to note here as Wallis-Budge points out that, in Egyptian mystical beliefs, recorded in the Papyrus of Ani and the Papyrus of Nesi-Amsu, the god Akeru also helps Horus and Ra to conquer the evil serpent, Apep. So the Akeru are important in the process of the soul after death finding its way beyond sinister, threatening beings to the light of Isis (or the divine feminine). But this same journey also applied to the acolyte in the Mysteries. So too, here at Lalibela, in the sacred landscape of the architecture, you cannot enter the house of Mary, the divine feminine, without going into the (little) house of the two lions.

So again a potent association with the ancient Egyptian sun god religion! But, what evidence exists that this conclusion may really be the case? Firstly, we recall that Lalibela is associated with the sun god in the legendary accounts of his life. This is indicated by his journeys to Heliopolis and Pythagoreans and to Zarathustrian sages.

These things seem to show that this remarkable king believed that the Christian religion involves the same deity as the sun god of Heliopolis. This probably caused Lalibela's view of Christianity to be deeply suspect to high ranking Ethiopian church leaders. But since he was the king, and had been through a remarkable spiritual experience, he was able to maintain his authority.

It certainly appears that on the sides of the western entrance to Biet Maryam the two helpers of the sun god (but here understood as a cosmic Christian deity) have been carved. For if a king orders the carving of these two lions at the entrance to the monument, and he has a link to the sun god religion of Heliopolis, then here we must have the Akeru, helpers of the sun god. And hence we find more evidence that Christ is viewed in some way as the sun spirit. And furthermore, this means that this house-like church, or spiritual residence, is dedicated to a greater being than the Virgin Mary. It is dedicated to something impersonal, possibly Sophia, as the symbol of purity and wisdom. What is the Sophia?

7A Left: The Akeru lions A colourized outline of the badly deteriorated carving of 2 lions at either side of the western entrance to Biet Maryam

These are now difficult to photograph, but still detectable to the eye under good observing conditions.

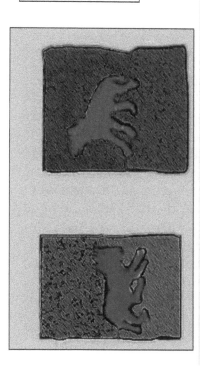

7B

The Akeru or two lion-sphinxes
On the stele between the paws of the sphinx. A dual representative of the sun-god Ra. Above them is the winged sun-disc.

The search for Isis or Sophia

The idea of a goddess of wisdom Sophia arose in the Hellenistic world, and is in essence based on the belief that when a person achieves great spiritual purity, and hence has the compassion and wisdom that spiritualization brings about, then something of the Divine lives in that person's soul. But in addition, it was felt that these finer soul qualities which the acolyte can acquire, derive from a spiritual being. These qualities were thought of as personalized or individuated in the form of a goddess, called Sophia.

The word Sophia came to mean both the quality of wisdom deriving from a pure heart and also the spiritual being whose nature is exactly this, and who inspired the striving acolyte in the Mysteries to reach for this higher state. In ancient Egypt the goddess Isis was this same goddess; the nature of the goddess Isis is such that she can be seen as a kind of Sophia. In earlier mystical Christian circles, the Virgin Mary was considered to be of such purity that the Sophia was present in her soul. But in addition, the Virgin Mary was viewed as a symbol of Sophia.

Now, the really significant point about this building at Lalibela is this underlying meaning; which exactly parallels the beliefs of the ancient Egyptians. Namely that the deceased soul on its journey up to the sun god realm is described as reaching a stage where, with the help of Horus, it can approach the House of Isis. But at this point we are told that, just in front of the house of Isis is located the House of Akeru, the double lion-god! So, in its journey after death, the soul of the dead has to first enter the house of the double lion-god Akeru, before it can enter the House of Isis (i.e., Sophia). Now this might seem irrelevant to understanding Lalibela, but in fact, in ancient religions, the pathway of the soul after death up through the seven heavens to Osiris, (or whatever the sun god was called in different countries) was exactly the same journey that the mystic underwent, on the journey up to the divine.

There is a notable saying about the symbiotic link of the death process and the initiation process, from Hellenistic Greek literature. It probably derives from the famous Greek historian Plutarch. He was a priest at the famous shrine of Delphi, so one may conclude that he had been initiated. These words are preserved in the writings of an anthologist, Johannes of Stobae (5th century AD), "The soul at death undergoes an experience similar to those who undergo great initiations…" (17)

In any event, this is what the Egyptian Book of the Dead says (78th chapter),

> "O Osiris, I shall come each day into the House of the double Lion-god and I shall {then} come forth from this place into the House of Isis, the divine woman." (18)

The soul of the dead hopes that the spiritualization process, which it naturally enters after death, will open up for it access to the realm of Isis or Sophia. But we have briefly noted that the after-death journey into spirit realms is regarded by mystics as being the same as that which is travelled by the acolyte in spiritual experiences. So, in other words, the acolyte in the initiatory process is also seeking the inner purity which opens the realm of Isis or Sophia to him or her, whilst they are still alive. **And this is the reason for these strange carvings here at Lalibela.** There definitely seems to be a connection between the Egyptian sun religion and Lalibela's Christianity. The carvings on the façade of Biet Maryam are connected with this Egyptian religious view, **because only by first passing through the house of the two lions can you enter the house of the Sophia.** You enter via the western porch, and in ancient Egypt the west is the direction from whence the Dead begin their journey; from the west bank of the Nile!

If you read the sacred landscape here, you discover Lalibela's message. Before attaining to the higher wisdom, symbolized by Isis or Sophia, (who helps create this new spirituality), one has to achieve the blessing of the sun god, (understood as a kind of cosmic Christ). So the acolyte in this remote sacred site, quietly contemplating these other-worldly ideas inside the still, dark spaces of the sanctuaries here, would face the question, "How do you get a link to the great sun god?"

The hint is given in the two lions; in ancient Egypt, various rituals and contemplations of the sun god Ra/Osiris would have been undertaken, in the quest for Isis. In the mystical striving of the ancient Egyptian acolytes, the rays streaming out from the sun god, symbolized by the dual-deity Akeru, were very important. For they are the symbol of the setting and the rising sun god.

But how did Lalibela think the acolyte at this unique site would unite with his cosmic version of Christ, the new sun god, who had visited the Earth? Somehow the Akeru lions, on the portals leading through into the house of Sophia were a guide in this quest. How could we understand this fascinating and beautiful Christian metamorphosis of the old Egyptian symbol today? Perhaps Lalibela's answer would be this: these two aspects of the sun god's rays (the 2 lions) are a poetic image of spiritual sunlight streaming into the soul, from the transcendent solar Christ, bringing about the dawn of the higher spiritual qualities in the acolyte.

Thus whoever seeks to truly become their higher self, following the teachings of Christ about manifesting selfless good-will to other people, will find that they are absorbing these rays. (And with this we are back to Origenes again!)

The sun god again: the Odes of Solomon
This is not actually a unique perspective, for as we saw earlier, the great 3rd century Christian, Origenes of Alexandria, also thought along these lines. He taught that the souls questing for spirituality are in fact absorbing non-physical light from 'the spiritual sun'. As we noted earlier, he puts his astounding holistic perspective like this. In his commentary on the Gospel of St. John he writes, 'For those for who do not take up into themselves the solar rays of the Christ, the apostles and prophets offer some (weaker) illumination'. (19) A remarkable

sentence, which shows that early Christians did have at least some kind of idea or poetic image of a cosmic solar Christ.

And there is another text, a rare text from the Hellenistic Age which is written in Greek called the Odes of Solomon, in which the divine is described as if it were a kind of spiritual equivalent of the sun. It appears to have its origins in initiatory Hebrew circles. It is not an orthodox religious text, and is in the form of poems of praise to the Divine (called *the Lord)*, in the manner of the Psalms. Only three of the 42 Odes have a definite reference to Christ, so it is very likely that this name was inserted in a later century by a Christian editor.

This fact shows however, that to this editor, the Christ was also seen as a solar being. The mystic who wrote the Odes Of Solomon states discreetly in Ode 15 that his Lord is actually the Sun. This may appear to be only a poetic image, but he goes on to say that from the rays of this (spiritual) sun he has been able to arise spiritually, and that his eyes derive from the sun:

> Just as the sun is a joy for those who are yearning for his day, so too, is the Lord my joy. For he is my sun, and his rays have raised me up; and his light has dispelled all darkness from my face. Through him I have acquired eyes, and have seen his holy day... (20)

These ideas from Origenes and the writer of the Odes, would have been quite at home in Heliopolis, in a ritual to the sun god Ra! Moreover, just as Isis was a helper to the sun god Osiris, so too the Virgin Mary was a helper and servant to the Messiah, as if she were a new form of the old goddess Isis. At least, long ago this is what people thought in Ethiopia, not just in Lalibela. Ethiopian Christians actually thought that there was a parallel between the Blessed Virgin Mary, (or rather the goddess inspiring her called Sophia), and the goddess Isis. There are indications of this in various old Ethiopian Christian texts, where Mary was seen in the role of representing Sophia; where she was seen as the equivalent of the goddess Isis.

For example, in the strange old Ethiopian book, the "Bandlet of Righteousness", also known as the Ethiopian Book of Life, various parallels between Mary (as a symbol of Sophia) and Isis are to be found. Mary seems to be more than human in this text, and she requires from Christ to know his secret name. Now this is just what we find in ancient Egyptian texts; Isis also makes great effort to find out the secret 'name of power' of the god Ra.

As the translator, Wallis-Budge, points out, Mary in this Ethiopian text has the same role for the souls of the dead, as Isis has for the souls of the dead in the Egyptian Book of the Dead. She helps to guide them up to the realm of the sun god. (21) It is intriguing to note here that the Gospel of St. Matthew also provides a link between Jesus and Egypt, in stating that when persecution by Herod threatened the safety of the child Jesus, **the family fled to Egyp**t. In non-Biblical texts, in the "Arabic Gospel of the Infancy" it is stated that the town to which the Holy Family actually travelled was called Matarea or Matarieh. But in fact, this is that very town sacred to sun god, which long ago was called **Heliopolis**! (22)

In any event at the Lalibela site, the pathway along its sacred landscape takes you firstly into the little house of the sun god assistants or mediators, (the Akeru), and only then can you enter the house of the Sophia (Biet Maryam). The message seems to be, if you wish to find your way to Sophia (previously known as Isis), you need the help of the sun god Christ (previously Ra), that is, the help of his rays of light (manifested by Akeru). Now of course this is radically different to any normal church symbolism, but the point is that here we have an initiatory site. This interpretation of these remarkable carvings is actually affirmed strongly by another strange, esoteric scene carved above the house of the Akeru, above its western porch.

Chapter Six: the mystic heart of this site

Above the Akeru porch of Biet Maryam: the initiatory challenge

Yet another potent statement about the mystical path and its challenges is to be found on the front of this church. Above the western entrance to Biet Maryam, now somewhat eroded, is a most intriguing carving, made in two sections. This scene, which is hard to make out today owing to deterioration of the volcanic rock, has been noted by only a few writers, as very few books have ever been written about Lalibela. Normally it is assumed that this double panel relief depicts St. George killing a dragon. So, one is told that it was carved long after the death of king Lalibela, in fact by the Portuguese in the 16th century.

Irmgard Bidder on the other hand, saw this as depiction of the Dioscuri, which are ancient Grecian twin deities, who carry out various heroic deeds. The German traveller Pfeiffer saw it as a reference to the Book of Revelation, in particular the brass rod of the high personage referred to the fourth letter to the churches. The official photographer Gerster saw in it a depiction of two Ethiopian equestrian saints, although he acknowledges that, in accordance with Ethiopian art traditions, there should be a halo for each of these two men. (23) He notes that in an old church at Asmara there is a wood-carving showing a mounted rider holding a sword in one hand, and what certainly appears to be a round shield in the other hand.

But all these assessments are incorrect. As we shall see, this artwork actually goes back to the 13th century when Lalibela was building the site, and is deeply mystical, it has nothing to with the St. George motif. So what does this scene depict? Not two horse riders, but the same solitary horse rider, shown twice. On the left, it shows the man on horseback with a lance or long spear, not a sword. Above him is the round circle, which we understand to be not a round shield, but rather the spiritual sun, see illustration 8.

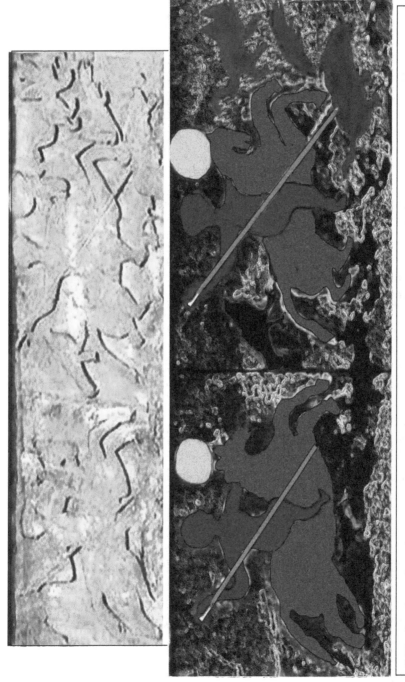

8 The deteriorated carving on the western façade of Biet Maryam A photo and a colour enhancement of features in the damaged double relief. Left: the spiritual journey has just begun. Right: later in the quest one encounters 3 beasts.

A mounted warrior with a sword may well carry a shield, but here the rider is in a scene which is about a spiritual encounter, not a normal battlefield. In the left scene, underneath the horse is a small eagle, only faintly visible now.

On the right scene, the same rider, with the spiritual sun above him, is shown again, but this time with a significant difference. The eagle has now risen up; it is now above the back of his horse. But as well, he is now confronted by three beasts. He is spearing one of these three beasts, or three monsters, which are in his way; and since he is not wielding a lance, a shield is not needed. Below is a kind of aquatic creature, somewhat above him is a crocodile monster, and further up is a leopard or a hyena.

The second panel on the left-hand side is saying that there is a task, a challenge to be completed, if the entry to this House of Mary is to be successful. The right-hand side is revealing what that task actually is: the Three Beasts have to be vanquished! At the Externsteine, the great Celtic site in Germany, there is a similar starkly admonishing scene, depicting a dragon coiled around a man and a woman. Here is something similar, but now the monster is triune. What are these three monsters? In literature from across the world, where the initiatory journey is the theme, the hero has to conquer three beasts, or a three-headed, or a beast composed of three monsters.

The Three Beasts: the great catharsis
In a great text from Celtic Europe prior to the Middle Ages, in the Epic of Beowulf, we find that Beowulf has to do battle with three monsters (Grendel, Grendel's mother, and the dragon). And in the Mabinogion, a mystical Welsh text, the hero Gwydion, has to do battle with three beasts, in a story involving shape-changing and various magical events. And in Christian Europe, about the time the monuments at Lalibela were being built, the poet Dante, wrote his remarkable epic, "The Divine Comedy"; a long poem about the journey of a soul into spirit realms, with a helper. (24)

In the section entitled, Hell, Canto 1, it is described how as he goes through the lower part of the Underworld Dante has to battle against three beasts: "a leopard, nimble and light and fleet ....a lion, swift and savage with head held high, and next a wolf, gaunt, with famished craving...". So, it becomes evident that the process of seeking the higher self involves an initial struggle against three beasts. The question then arises, why the number three?

In ancient Greece the hero Bellerophon on his winged steed, Pegasus, has to fight against the Chimera, a terrible monster composed of three separate beasts with the body and maned head of a lion, a goat's head rising from its back, a set of goat-udders, and a serpentine tail. In Grecian legends about Hercules, it is said that he has to battle against three-headed dog, Cerberus, with three heads and three sets of legs all joined at the waist. It is also said that Cerberus guards the entrance to the Underworld.

It is usually said in ancient myths that the heroes encountered these three beasts, or a threefold beast, at the entrance to the Underworld. As we have noted throughout our explorations of the sacred sites, this is the same realm as Sheol or Hades, the realm of the dead. So why do these old initiates, (called heroes) have to battle with a triune monster? Another graphic Egyptian image gives an answer as to just why the acolytes in the Mysteries of olden times had to encounter the triune beast. This image from the Egyptian Book of the Dead is part of a larger artwork which shows the process that occurs to a person after their death.

The heart of the deceased is being weighed in the scales, against a white feather that represents spiritual goodness and truth. To the far right of this weighing of the heart, there sits a remarkable monster. It is a triune beast, and it is eagerly waiting, see illustration 9. It is waiting to devour as much of the deceased's soul as it is allowed, i.e., as much of it as is unethical. The beast, called Amemet, is literally a triune monster, one third hippopotamus, one third crocodile and one third lion. It is made up of three beasts, similar to what is carved on the Lalibela church, but compressed into one entity; this combined beast is a variant that is mentioned in initiatory stories.

Now we noted earlier that the spiritual journey involves going through the same processes as experienced by those who have died. The Egyptian triune monster in the Underworld mentioned in the Book of the Dead is the same sinister force which heroes such as Hercules and Gwydion had to encounter whilst on the Earth. The question arises, why does the acolyte encounter three beasts or a threefold beast? No specific explanation of this seems to have been written by the ancients; but we note that in the Egyptian Book of the dead, the Egyptian triune beast, called Amemet, is a symbol of the mind or soul of the deceased person. So it has to represent the evil side of the soul, of consciousness. (25) So, the threefold theme must reflect three primary strands of the soul itself, see illustration 10.

It is of course quite common to regard human consciousness as twofold, namely as 'head and heart', i.e., the emotions and logic. But it is also possible to see this definition as a bit incomplete, in so far as we do have a third capacity, namely the volitional power or will. So what are the Three Beasts? This is no doubt a wide variety of possible answers, drawn from a long list of ethical defects that may lurk in the soul. But it appears that on the wall of the Biet Maryam, inspired by special wisdom that Lalibela obtained in his out-of-body experience, the negative side of the emotions, of intelligence, and of the will are being presented as obstacles to overcome.

64

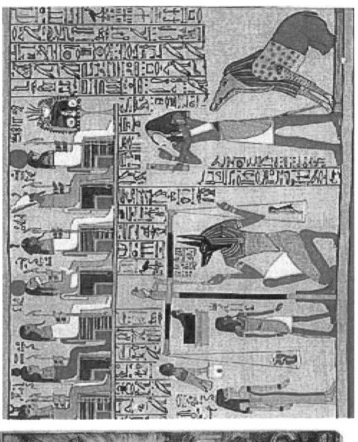

9 The 3 Beasts Hercules fighting Bellerophon & the triune beast in the Netherworld from an Egyptian Book of the Dead.

10 The 3 Beasts in Dante A medieval depiction of Dante meeting the 3 beasts

A scene similar to the mystical carvings above the entrance to Biet Maryam. (colourized by author)

In Dante's Divine Comedy, the lion represents pride, the leopard represents decadent desires, and the she-wolf represents violence and fear. Probably the three beasts at Lalibela represent something similar, with a specific focus on the spiritual challenges awaiting the acolyte. There is an interesting link here with the initiatory Egyptian cult of Serapis, which came into prominence in the Hellenistic era; Serapis (or Sarapis) was in effect a new form of the sun cult of Osiris.

It is known that in the temple of this Egyptian god, at Alexandria, next to a statue of the god himself, there was a statue of a three headed beast; consisting of wolf, lion and dog. (26) We can also note that in terms of Biblical ideas, there are also the three beasts mentioned in the Book of Jeremiah (5:6), beasts that are to fall upon Israel because of their sins. But here at Lalibela, the scene is about the individual on the quest for spirituality, not the over-all community.

Summing up, one could conclude that this carving is a message to the acolyte to be aware that, as part of the spiritual illumination process, there will be an encounter with the still-untransformed lower drives. As this encounter happens, the sun-spirit will be there as a guide and helper, but even so the acolyte will have to confront the three lower shadows of the soul. This encounter can unleash a storm of negative energies, which the acolyte then has to conquer; it is called The Dark Night of the Soul. In other words, this carving above the western porch of Biet Maryam is a stern admonition to spiritualize the intellect, the feelings and the intentions (or will).

Lalibela's private contemplation cell

These remarkable carvings which are directly related to initiatory processes, were regarded by Lalibela as so vital to the site, that a special contemplation space was carved out of the trench wall opposite, to allow a person to focus on them.

In the western wall of the courtyard or trench surrounding Biet Maryam, a special monk's cell was carved out, several metres above the ground level; it is accessible by some stone steps. From this place, facing towards the western porch of the church, an acolyte could directly gaze out at these carvings. This appears to be the esoteric heart of the site. It is said by commentators that this contemplation cell was designed to help king Lalibela gaze down on religious ceremonies occurring in the trench courtyard below. But it is much more likely that the primary function was to facilitate contemplation of the carvings.

It appears that the intention of Lalibela in designing this feature was to remind an acolyte, as he entered Biet Maryam, to bear in mind that, although for the wider community its purpose is to encourage reverence for the Virgin Mary, its esoteric purpose was something else. This deeper purpose was to contemplate that the sinister three beasts appear on the western wall, the furthest from the rising of the sun. The shadow side of the triune soul, its emotions, its thoughts and its intentions, have to be conquered before the soul becomes the house of Sophia. We conclude that the purpose of the sanctuary is to encourage and admonish the acolyte to strive to make their soul into a tabernacle for the Sophia. So what is inside this remarkable building?

Inside Biet Maryam

Inside the church, which is the only fully decorated church in the entire Lalibela site, one finds lovely devotional frescoes on Biblical themes associated with the Virgin Mary; such as her meeting with Elizabeth, the mother of John the Baptist. There is also a great array of patterns and geometrical figures either painted on the ceilings or carved onto the walls and pillars, but in fact, there is very little mystical imagery. There is a double-headed eagle, and a fresco of two bulls fighting, and the six-pointed star, amongst other simple ornamental motifs. What does stand out is the profusion of circular designs with three concentric spheres, in the centre of which is a star-like object.

In addition, a yellow circle with a face in it is very noticeable; but just what it depicts is unclear.

The nature of the drawing is not quite compatible stylistically with other works of art in the church. It is possibly the sun, but depicted as a living entity. Of course, the depiction of Christ as the sun can also be an expression of a purely symbolic-poetic view of Christ. But since the entire site itself is dedicated to Christ, who was seen by Lalibela as in some way similar to the revered sun spirit of ancient Egypt, it is not impossible that this face was mean to depict a sun spirit.

There is also a cloth-covered pillar inside this church. The legends of Lalibela's life recount that one day when he was deep in sacred contemplation, the risen Jesus Christ appeared to him, and stretched forth his hand towards him, before disappearing. This happened near the pillar which is now covered with cloth; it is understood that after this vision, Lalibela had a text carved into the column, in which he expresses his core spiritual message. But the pillar is always left veiled.

Two travellers' reports from the 1940-1050's give a fine impression of the ambience which permeated these buildings for about 800 years, and which is still there today, to some extent. The British social activist, Sylvia Plankhurst, who engaged strongly with Ethiopia, as part of her anti-colonialist stance, reported from the 1950's in her book, Ethiopia a Cultural History,

> Mariam is alone at Lalibela in having three exterior porches built out from the main fabric {of the building}. Above the west porch is a bas-relief of two equestrian figures -- engaged in combat with a dragon {sic}. The interior is richly decorated -- with highly conventionalized ornament: foliage, birds and animals, the two-headed eagle and other symbols frequently used in early Christian art, with frets, key-patterns and interlacing patterns. The cross is frequently introduced.

Mariam has a nave and two aisles formed by two rows of five rectangular piers. In the centre of the transept is a tall central pier which helps to support the barrel-vault of the nave. There are three chapels at the east end, each with its altar. The capitals, which extend slightly beyond the top of the pier, are cubical but slightly concave, a feature emphasized by the ornament. In place of the abacus the capital is surmounted by four brackets, each an oval moulding surmounting one face of the capital. These brackets are richly ornamented." (27)

And the artist Beatrice Playne reported from the late 1940's, from her time in Biet Maryam,

The interior is very small and so hung with curtains that it is difficult to see much of it. When I got used to the darkness I was aware that the architraves, soffits and capitals, and even some of the pillars themselves, were beautifully carved with interlacing, Celtic-like patterns, and that parts of the ceiling and of the walls carried fragments of fresco. It looked as if the entire ceiling had once been covered...

On entering the west doorway...one is confronted by a pillar which more or less screens the interior and which is normally kept veiled. It was now uncovered for my benefit and revealed a Madonna and Child, with a prostrate donor under her feet, painted in tempera on cloth attached to the pillar itself.

Although I thought that it was unlikely that this painting was earlier than late seventeenth or even eighteenth century, it had great dignity of pose and richness of colouring. The elaborateness of the costume and its various details, gave it an extremely oriental appearance which could easily have come through Goanese influence brought in by Jesuit missionaries."

I had forgotten how very small the interior was and how very dark. The stone porches before each of the three doors cut out most of the light and it takes a long time before one's eyes can pick out the details of the decoration. This is much more elaborate in Mariam than in any of the other Lalibela churches...

(28)

It is now time to walk along further, past the church of Maryam, to the next fascinating monument.

Chapter Seven: A global temple for the Community of Goodwill

Medhanie Alem: sanctuary for the 72 nations

From the church of Maryam, (or the Sanctuary of the Sophia), a narrow trench leads on to the splendid sanctuary of Medhanie Alem, which means, the church of the Saviour of the World. But by now we have journeyed to the easternmost boundary of the site. This is the direction which represents the sun, and hence in old mystical traditions, the sun spirit. It appears that Medhanie Alem is a sanctuary dedicated to this Christianized sun spirit. So what sort of building is this?

It is the largest, and most striking, of the 10 sanctuaries. It is also **the largest monolithic rock-hewn church in the world**, measuring about 12 metres high, 12 wide and 12 long, and situated in an excavated courtyard some 33.5m x 23.5m; the building itself is standing on a plinth, and covers an area of almost 800m^2. A description of the interior is given from the primary tourist website about Lalibela, http://www.selamta.net/lalibela.htm;

> Around the high walls of the nave runs a frieze of blind windows framed by protruding beams at each corner. Along the sides, the windows are either blind windows with decorations or actual openings between the "galleries" and the nave. The "galleries" can be reached from a cell to the left of the narthex.

> One particular pillar in the centre is covered with a cloth. This is the "amd", meaning the symbol of the unity of faith. The priests explain that Christ touched the pillar when appearing to King Lalibela in one of his later visions, after the sanctuary had been built. Since that time the past and the future of the world are written on it. Since man is too weak to bear the truth revealed by God the pillar is covered. In the nave, the shafts, capitals and corbels of the columns and pilasters as well as the arches are carved in bas-relief, and some of them are painted.

What is significant here, in terms of a conscious architectural design or language, is that the monument has 72 four-sided (rectangular) pillars. Its substantial roof is held up by a veritable forest of pillars on the inside, in four rows, and there is a colonnade of more pillars around the outside perimeter, see illustration 11.

One gains the impression that the large number of pillars is really significant, that is beyond pragmatic architectural requirements, because they severely reduce the space available for any sizeable gathering inside. The external pillars being quite slender, are not very robust, and in fact some had to be replaced in the 1950's.

A significant point about this sanctuary is the number 72, and the fact that the number four is present in a variety of ways. There is a door on the west, south and north sides, whilst on the eastern side, the solar side, there is an altar, above which is a dome. The external pillars are rectangular in their profile, as we noted earlier, so this means that the pillars of the church, are, very unusually, four sided.

So, in terms of architecture, the building's three doors and its altar create an internal cross shape, with its four parts, whilst all around the outside perimeter, 36 four-sided pillars encompass the monument. To carve 72 slender columns, each with a square profile, is a demanding task.

We can conclude that to Lalibela this temple represents the many diverse nations and ethnicities of humanity, being united in a community of brotherhood and sisterhood. A community that Lalibela felt could arise, when due to the spiritual activity of this cosmic Christ, good-will is empowered in the human heart.

11 **Medhanie Alem, the sanctuary of the Savior of the World.** A deeply mystical design, it is a temple symbolizing the global community of good-will

For the number 72 is not a haphazard number. In Hebrew and Christian mystical Biblical texts it is the number of humanity itself. It is regarded as the number of nations created by God. Of course there are many more nations than 72, but to the ancient Hebrew mystics, there were 72 primary nations on the Earth, from which all the others have their origin. It is the number of the nations that form the underlying group structure of all humanity so to speak. The underlying number of nations from which other nations have developed in the course of time.[iii]

And these 72 nations were each viewed as having a spiritual counterpart to them. Both Biblical texts and non-Biblical spiritual texts refer to these nations as each having a spirit being ministering to them; a kind of national spirit, and these are known collectively as "the 72 princes on high". (29) The early Ethiopian church was very aware of this theme, and indeed the rest of general theological knowledge and currents elsewhere in Christendom, despite its isolation. The church was well informed about such themes; it is reported that the church possessed very substantial libraries of theological books.

For example, the church collection included a very comprehensive and respected theological encyclopaedia from medieval times, called the al-Hawi or Pandektaes. In addition, amongst other documents, in an Ethiopian church library there is a chronological listing of the 81 patriarchs of the church in the Egyptian city of Alexandria, the historical data in this is described as "astoundingly exact" by the German scholars who inspected it. (30)

And there is evidence that the theme of the 72 Disciples of Christ had been the subject of interest in Ethiopian theology, also. For example, a document exists in a monastery on Lake Tana in which these 72 people have been given specific names, indicating a considerable interest in this theme. (31) It appears that this view of 72 nations lies behind the mysterious reference in the New Testament to the other apostles, a second group, who were sent out as missionaries by Christ, in addition to the 12 disciples, in Luke 10:1,

> After this the Lord appointed seventy-two others and sent them two by two ahead of him to every town and place where he was about to go. [iv]

It is very probable that this number 72 is an allusion to this primal number of the core nations, each with their own national spirit. This interpretation seems confirmed when a mystical Christian text is considered, which specifically refers to 72 nations. This text is the Gospel of Philip, which contains a mixture of material. It contains some valid material from the beginning of the Christian era, and some later, more theoretical material of lesser value. This book indicates through a parable (63:26-30) that Christ will somehow bring a harmonizing between the different peoples, creating social bonds of community between them, the implication being that this will form humanity into a unified brotherhood and sisterhood:

> The Lord (Jesus) went into the dye works of Levi. He took 72 different colours and threw them into the vat. Then he took them out, all neutral cloth-coloured. And he said, "Even so has the Son of Man come as a dyer." (32)

In other words, the different nations of the world shall, in some future era all become merged into a unifying common group. So, what is the message in the architecture of Medhanie Alem, the foremost sanctuary at Lalibela, with its 72 four-sided columns and four cardinal points inside? The 72 columns represent all the nations of humanity; the four sided structure of the columns is echoed inside by the four cardinal points on the inside created by the three doors and the eastern altar, which together form a cross.

The sanctuary itself is placed the furthest to the east of any monument, the rising point of the sun; all of these features are creating a message. It seems that this remarkable African king concluded from his mystical experience, that new spiritual energies are available to humanity as a result of the Christ sacrifice at Golgotha. Perhaps the idea behind this monument is that Lalibela thought that subtle spiritual energies were now available which could provide the basis for social harmony amongst all the various nations.

In any event, it appears that the structure of this sanctuary is a meditation in stone, in which Lalibela was saying to his acolytes, 'Here is a symbol of humanity from the four corners of the world, who are now able to be harmoniously united. Since the events of Golgotha, because of the descent of the great sun spirit, they can become imbued with spiritual energies, unifying people of goodwill.' This is presumably what the advent of Christ meant to Lalibela, whom he viewed as a cosmic being, the sun spirit; that same unifying solar divinity venerated at Heliopolis and Giza, and revered by Pythagoras and by Zarathustra.

We may never know this for sure, but it appears likely that Lalibela considered that there is now a new dynamic for humanity; at least for those who do seek social unity and are of good-will. Something like this underlies the design of this remarkable site. The original entrance to this group of monuments was from the west, passing the hollow block of Adam's Grave, and walking towards the east. But today the courtyard is entered from the south, as a new entrance has been made, connected by the trench leading to the sanctuary of Mary. This is certainly more convenient, but the underlying message of the walking meditation is lost, if one goes through the site in this way.

So summing up, we can conclude that despite a few minor architectural features possibly deriving from a time later than Lalibela's lifetime, the northern side of the site shows a grand mystical design. This would have to stem from Lalibela, as no other Ethiopian ruler of long ago is credited with such a visionary plans as the result of an out-of-body experience, see illustration 12.

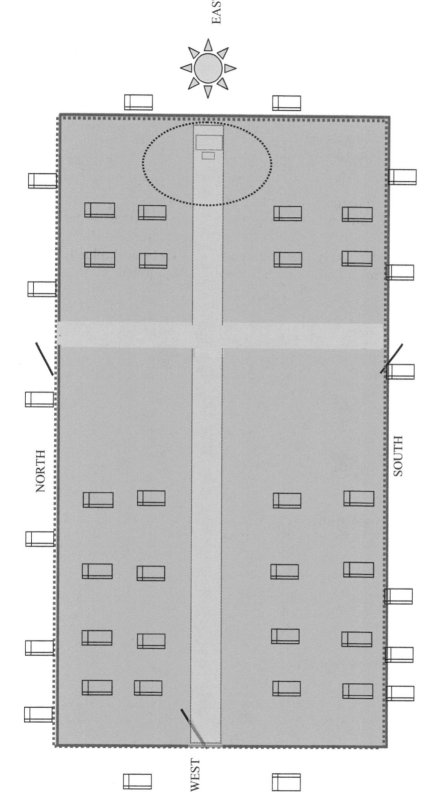

EAST

NORTH

SOUTH

WEST

12   **Medhanie Alem** The church of the Saviour of the World, or **The Sanctuary of the global Community of Goodwill.**

The Zagwe dynasty eventually lost its hold on Ethiopia, and power returned to the Axumite rulers, who suppressed reference to these usurpers. But there is evidence as Michael Gervers points out, that in the 15th century the Zagwean rulers, including Lalibela were rehabilitated after a period of being ignored.

It may then have happened that the new ruling dynasty decided to strengthen the charisma of Lalibela, as an affirmation of faith for their people, and at this time, some features of the over-all site were altered, to create a uniform legend. It is very likely that monument 11 (Gabriel/Raphael) and 12 (Mercurios) were transformed into churches at this time.

Chapter Eight: The Southern Side of Lalibela

Biet Emmanuel

The second group of sanctuaries or monuments is to the south of the dividing waterway called the river Jordan; see illustration 3. In this section of the site there is a natural fissure in the volcanic rock (called tuffa), and a hill has been cut in two by a deep trench, ending in a small hillock. This hillock has an underground tunnel leading to a small sanctuary at its top. The monuments here are arranged in a complex haphazard way; access to the various sanctuaries is either by underground tunnels or by log bridges laid over trenches. Here we need to notice that only no. 8 (the church of Emmanuel) and no. 9 (the church of Abba Libanos) are properly formed and oriented churches; the other monuments are radically different. In fact they were not built by Lalibela.

The most noticeable church here is Bet Emanuel, or the Church of Emanuel. Although there are no noticeable mystical features to this monument, we will consider it briefly, as it was the church used by Lalibela himself,

> Art historians consider Bet Emanuel to be the finest and most impressive church in Lalibela. Looked at from above, its mighty, flat-pitched roof can be seen glistening from the rock cradle that houses the church. It is the only true monolithic structure of this group, carefully sculptured from a block 18 x 12 x 12 m. The church offers an almost classic example of Axumite style despite the fact that the floor and side plans follow the true basilica pattern with a proper east-west orientation.

> Entering the courtyard you will see this fascinating church on its stepped platform shining in the bright red colour of the Lalibela tuffa. The imitation of Axumite wood and stone construction is striking, its walls built in horizontal and vertical bands, alternately recessed and projecting.

A rock staircase leads from a side room by the main entrance to a second storey; here little rock chambers surround the hall. The striking interior feature is the double frieze of blind windows in the vaulted nave, the lower frieze being purely ornamental, the upper one consisting of windows alternating with decorated areas. In the rock floor of the southern aisle a hole opens into a long, subterranean tunnel leading to neighbouring Bet Mercurios. (see www.selamta.net)

What is not mentioned in this description is the really curious fact that this church, like all the others, is sited inside a deep trench, but this monument was not accessible in any ordinary sense, unless some sort of rope ladder, about 11 metres long, was used! Access in Lalibela's time for the king was by one of three tunnels that led from his residence in Mercurios, across to the church. Mercurios was probably used in Lalibela's time as his royal palace and administrative centre.

But one of these tunnels opens out onto the southern wall of the trench so high up, that a ladder would be needed. One has to conclude with regard to the church, as well so many others monuments here, that it was important that access was made by subterranean tunnels. Just what perspective underlies this architectural feature, remains a mystery.

The other church is dedicated to Abba Libanos, and it appears that he was the genius responsible for the hydrology of the site; that is, for ensuring that the artesian water basin was accessed for use at the site, and indeed to create a reliable water flow for the many small farms which dot the countryside around Lalibela, see illustration 13. Inside the church there is a painting of him, with a cane pointing to a mountain top (Lalibela is high up on a plateau in the foothills of the Lasta mountain range). Where he touches the mountain, a water spring gushes forth; this is probably to symbolize his work in accessing the water, but it also may alludes to the story of Moses who touched a rock with his staff, and water miraculously gushed forth. The water for the churches here has to come from wells dug deep enough to give water in the dry season, and to provide enough water to run down the hills to the many small farms below. (33)

The House of Bread

There is also the curious artificial round building with the subterranean tunnel winding its way up inside the earth, and terminating in a small room, called "Bet Lehem", which we noted above. Here again www.selamta.net is informative,

> You may reach Bet Lehem by a passageway 50 m long that starts at the right-hand aisle of Bet Emanuel, and passes Bet Mercurios and the courtyard of Abba Libanos. The shrine has been shaped into a cone by the central trench: the tunnel winds up in spiral form within the hill and ends in a low, round room. A tree-trunk in the room serves as a central pillar. The original function of this shrine is not known. Visitors may not be allowed to enter the interior of Bet Lehem.

This mysterious chamber, called locally the Faras Bet, is open to the daylight, having some small openings cut into its upper part. This feature is not mentioned in the semi-legendary life of Lalibela, but it is only a small monument. This feature has several names, the Hill of Bread, the Bakery of the Holy Bread, the Stable of Lalibela's Horse, and the Hermit Cell of King Lalibela. However, it is unlikely that there were bakeries in Ethiopia at that time. Furthermore this room could never be a horse stable, nor did Lalibela ever dwell there; his palace very likely was what is now called the Church of Mercurios.

But, in any event, this room has to do with the theme of food; the question is, was it for the preparation or storing of the sacred host (Eucharistic bread) to be used in the church service. If so, it may also have been used for contemplations about 'food for the spirit', not actual food, but the spiritual 'bread of life'. The gospel saying of the Saviour (John 6: 48-50), was no doubt seen by Lalibela as meaning sustenance for the soul from a cosmic Christ:

13 **Abba Libanos** The church of Saint Libanos .Libanos developed the water reticulation system that provides the site with fresh water.

"I am the bread of life. Your forefathers ate the manna in the desert, yet they died. But here is the bread that comes down from heaven, which a person may eat and not die."

So this underground chamber, with a large tree trunk acting as a central pillar, may have been used in connection with a ritual or meditation associated with the mystical concept of the cosmic Christ as the bread of life; this is of course, in general terms, the central theme of the Mass or Eucharist service in any church. But since this site has a mystical basis to it, Lalibela may have widened the sacred theme of the church service to focus on the cosmic sun god 'Christ' as the spiritual source of the higher self. There are similar statements to be found in other religions about the sun spirit. Especially in ancient Egyptian texts about Horus, the representative of the sun god Ra, who presumably was to Lalibela, the prototype of Jesus. For Horus, too, both gives, and is, the spiritual bread of life,

"I am the lord of cakes in Annu (Heliopolis), and my bread is in heaven with Ra...   I am the creator of divine food...I am the divine food which is not corrupted..." (34)

Other features of this side of the site have little or nothing to do with Lalibela. They have a pre-Christian quality. The next feature in this southern group of monuments is the unusual twin 'church' of Gabriel and Raphael (these are two archangels prominent in Hebrew mystical texts), but it was certainly not a church originally. Again, selamta.net describes its general situation well:

The church is usually entered from the top of the rock near Bet Emanuel in the east, by a small bridge of logs leading over the central trench. You may also approach from the east by a series of small tunnels, or a gallery-like passage and another log bridge 10m above the courtyard. The triangular floor of the northern courtyard is enclosed by walls whence, high up, the facade of the church and the gallery opposite can be seen. Down in the courtyard there is a well and an underground cistern. Steps lead down to a subterranean hall of pillars, where the water sinks or rises, according to the dry and rainy seasons. (selamta. net)

Gabriel and Raphael: once a non-Christian sacred site?
This complex part of the site was not built by Lalibela; these ancient monuments were here before him. After his life-time, perhaps in a period when his contributions to Ethiopian church history were being re-affirmed, these old monuments were altered to form an unusual double chapel. A rock wall on the edge of the twin church, on the far left of the diagram (feature PH), leads up to the roof of the monument. This walkway is called 'the Path to Heaven' because when seen from below, the wall of this inclined walkway has what looks like seven blind (or false) doors carved into it. Now since the buildings here were not built by Lalibela, we can ask, what is being symbolized?

These seven arches or blind doors are actually an older Ethiopian symbol, derived from Axumite architecture, which created the round-headed shapes, often in the form of obelisks. They are to be found around Axum as stelas, or steles, i.e., upright stones, such as one finds at the Megalithic sites in Carnac and Britain, but these are more ornate. The impression one gets of such a form is that it represents the heavenly realms; it points upwards, see illustration 14.

In Egypt the early pyramids were step pyramids, they were not smooth-sided; they had seven distinct levels to them, admonishing the populace to think of the seven heavens, and the journey after death. We conclude that these seven blind doors, which probably date from around 600 AD, are really symbolizing the seven heavens, indicating that, prior to Lalibela, the Ethiopian church once had a centre here. But, in fact there may have been a pagan sacred site here, which could go back to pre-Christian times, and which the church specifically took over.

14 **The Path to Heaven** A walkway with 7 openings, like doorways. This was made some centuries before Lalibela. Below this is the ancient pagan water site

Roha Al-Ruha Place of Water

The area now called Lalibela was earlier called Roha, and scholars believe that this name comes from the Arabic term, Al-Ruha, which indicates a place of water. The question arises as to whether this feature, listed as no. 11 in our diagram, derives from indigenous Christian Ethiopian ideas or from a non-Christian spirituality. The question can perhaps be answered by noting that below the seven doors is the sunken concourse.

This is an area which has a specific connection to water which we mentioned earlier, see illustration 3, feature "C". Here the floor is far enough down into the plateau to reach the artesian water supply; there is a well and several cisterns. This can be looked upon as simply a water supply feature, but Bidder reports that there are steps leading down into a small hall of columns, submerged columns!

And when the wet season arrives, the water rises up to the floor of the concourse, because the site is built over natural springs. Further, in what is now the church of Gabriel there are a number of holes, mostly covered over, some of which go down a very long way, deep into the ground. There are also water drains set into the floor of the so-called church. Furthermore, there are two doors cut into the northern wall of this church, which lead nowhere, except to a short rock platform for each door, from which one gazes down below into the sunken concourse and its wells.

Now, a number of the churches here do have their own cistern, but to have the floor of a building so designed as to allow water to flood in and then drain out, is neither suitable for a church, nor is it part of the features of any pragmatic water supply. So the building may have once been a pagan temple designed to both give access to water, and to venerate water-spirits.

This is quite likely, as the indigenous people of Ethiopia, with whom the Axumites mingled, were the Agao (or Cushites).

They are known to have had a worship of nature-spirits and sky-spirits, but in particular, they venerated water-spirits who dwell in springs. (35) It is hard to escape the conclusion that there once existed here an ancient Agao-Axumite sacred site, dedicated to the water-spirits of the springs. Lalibela would have ignored this aspect of the monuments, and it was probably not used at all by him. It is however interesting that an earlier pagan sacred site was chosen as the site for mystical Christian purpose.

Summing up

We have now explored the many features of this site, and found that it is a mystical site, like those of Egypt or the Celts and the Megalithic builders, but one that derives from an unorthodox view of the Christian religion. Its isolation in the Ethiopian highlands, far from western Christendom, especially from Rome, meant that it was politically safe and culturally possible to construct such a site. Lalibela appears to be the only substantial Christian Mystery centre in the medieval world.

Finally, it should be mentioned that there are other features to this site that we have not explored, including the more traditional religious features of a church setting, such as paintings and relief carvings. Today the Lalibela churches are used as traditional Ethiopian churches; they are not empty disused sites through which tourists can wander at will. There are several hundred people being trained as priests, so it is a site that is venerated and in use. When visiting the site, one has to be respectful of this fact, and discreet in the endeavour to explore the fascinating qualities of the area.

Appendices

More About: reports and books on Lalibela

Although few books have ever been written about Lalibela, a number of books and academic articles have been written about Ethiopia in general, and these can have informative chapters on Lalibela. Some of the most informative include:

I. Bidder, Lalibela the monolithic churches of Ethiopia, Cologne 1958,
H. Dabbert, Die monolithenen Kirchen Lalibelas in Äthiopien, Berlin 1938,
Louis Findlay, *The Monolithic Churches of Lalibela in Ethiopia*, Cairo, 1944
G Gerster, Kirchen im Fels, Stuttgart 1968. An English trans. by Richard Hosking, *Churches in Rock. Early Christian Art in Ethiopia*, Phaidon, London, 1970
T.A. Lambie, A doctor without a country, New York c. 1940;
Sylvia Plankhurst Ethiopia, A Cultural History, Essex, Lalibela House, 1955
Beatrice Playne: St. George for Ethiopia, Constable, London, 1954
Anna-Lena Röstin, Arvet i Främlingars Hand, Bibeltrogna Vänners Förlag, Stockholm 1936

More recently, Stuart Munro-Hay (with P. Taor) in his book, **Ethiopia, the Unknown Land**, has a valuable chapter on Lalibela that is based on his extensive knowledge of over-all Ethiopian cultural history. His book provides a really excellent guide to the history and culture of Ethiopia. But his perspective does not consider the mystical nature of this site, which as we have seen, has been interwoven into its ecclesiastical character.

Michael Gervers has an excellent academic treatise on a part of the site,[v] but again the mystical intention underlying the site is not encompassed and hence conclusions are naturally drawn which are not necessarily accurate with respect to the underlying reason for the site. Ethiopia actually has a very valuable tradition of Christian knowledge and ancient texts, some of which had disappeared from every other part of the Christian world. Ethiopia has also had a long tradition of a more holistic, mystical approach to Christianity, in which spiritual beings and spiritual realms are naturally integrated.

The Deutschen Morgenländischen Gesellschaft (The German Oriental Society), after an extensive research program undertaken in Ethiopia to ascertain what religious documents were preserved there published a catalogue, listing Ethiopian religious writings, through Ernst Hammerschmidt. This shows the valuable role played by the Ethiopian church in preserving Christian texts known in the West and the more mystical initiatory type of religious document. A very useful description of all the monuments, from a purely descriptive viewpoint, is available on the Internet at, http://www.selamta.net/lalibela.htm.

More About: the 40 year cycle
A list of Ethiopian monarchs shows most of them ruling for 40 years; which is very unlikely to be an historically true account. At 40 yrs of age, Moses struck the Egyptian overseer and fled away; he remained 40 yrs outside of Egypt before he returned to take Israelites out. He then spent 40 years wandering in the desert. And before being given the 10 commandments, he remained on top of Mount Horeb for 40 days.

It appears that the number 40 signified to the ancient Hebrew mystics the completion of a cycle in which something significant is achieved. The Ethiopian church felt very closely linked to the Hebrew era, hence the feature of having a simple wooden object that represents the Ark of the Covenant in their churches. And no doubt also this led to them using the 40 year cycle in their own chronicles.

More About: No evidence of Templar Knights in Ethiopia
The claim that Knights Templar were involved in the building
of Lalibela is based primarily on a careless approach to a
passage in an old semi-historical, semi-hearsay text about
Ethiopia, written by a certain Abu Salih, dating from about
1210 AD. In New Ages circles the rumour has been spread
that he describes a religious procession in Ethiopia attended by
king Lalibela, and that amongst the attendants present were
some men who were "white and red in complexion, with pale
hair". Since such persons would not be of the native African
stock, this is presented as evidence of the presence of Knights
Templar; and that perhaps they helped build the Lalibela
churches.

Fortunately, reliable material about Ethiopia and its religious
significance (especially in regard to the Ark of the Covenant)
is given in the book, "The Ark of the Covenant; the true story
of the greatest relic of antiquity", by R. Grierson and S.
Munro-Hay, two academically competent experts. They reveal
the truth about this quote, namely that the 13th century report
by Salih states that present at the festival were, "both Lalibela
himself and some others {all of whom} were white and red in
complexion, with pale hair". So it has nothing whatsoever to
do with some strangers from Europe, for obviously it
specifically **includes** king Lalibela. (36) But why would this
be said of king Lalibela?

It has its reason in a particular attitude of all Ethiopian
dynasties concerning the majesty and sacred lineage of their
kings. They declared themselves to be "Solomonic" kings
(i.e., descended from king Solomon), because of the very
prominent Hebrew (or Old Testament) orientation of
Ethiopian Christianity. In the case of the Zagwean dynasty to
which Lalibela belongs, this was an even more emotive issue,
as this dynasty had seized power from another dynasty whose
claim to be of Solomonic origin was based on a long-
established theme, whereas the Zagweans in their ancestry
actually lacked the required lineage which could give a basis
for this proud claim.

They had to resort to a lesser genealogical lineage, and so it was only natural that in any reports of their life and official deeds, there would be indications and hints that the king and others of his family were indeed also Solomonic descendants of the Israelites. One way to do this is to hint at non-African racial features. Of course Semitic people would have these paler colour tones, as they were not of African stock. It is not impossible that some of the Knights Templar did visit Lalibela, just as there were Ethiopian priests who were deputized to travel to Europe at times. But the above passage from Abu Salih cannot be used as evidence for Templar knights visiting Lalibela at all.

Very few European people made visits to Lalibela in the medieval period, and there is no evidence of members of the Knights Templar Order being in Lalibela and helping in the construction of the churches.[vi] There is a rumour, recorded by the missionary Francisco Alvarez, who visited there in ca. 1520, that the Ethiopians believe that "the site was made by white men, and that the first Christian king (Lalibela) of this country was a stranger." But this is self-evidently a reference to the attitude put forward strongly by the Zagwean kings that they also were of Semitic origin.

REFERENCES

1 G Gerster, Kirchen im Fels, Stuttgart 1968. (English version: Churches in Rock), Phaidon, London, 1970, p 86.

2 Stuart Munro-Hay & Pamela Taor, Ethiopia, the Unknown Land, I.B.Tauris, 2002 p. 195.

3 Reflections on Christianity: Two Perspectives on Ethiopia's Living Tradition, Alisa LaGamma; Chester Higgins, Jr. photographer http://www.metmuseum.org/education /er_lecture_archive/sam_cia/lagamma_page_7.asp

4 New York Times Thursday July 9 2009

5 The Dictionary of Ethiopian Biography, ed. M. Belaynesh, S. Chopjnacki, R. Pankhurst, Addis Ababa, Institute of Ethiopian Studies Ad. Ab. Univ. 1975

6 The Gadl or Gerla Lalibela
Parts of this legend, preserved in the Ethiopian language of Ge'ez, are presented in English in various histories of Ethiopia: Taddesse Tamrat, Church and State in Ethiopia, Clarendon press (Oxford 1972), and in K.P. Pankhurst The Ethiopian Royal Chronicles OUP, Addis Abeba, 1967. Significant extracts from the Gadl or Gerla are also preserved in Portuguese, in the detailed report about Ethiopia written in 1607 by a Jesuit priest, Pedro Paez, from his visit there, published as "Historia Aethiopiae", "in Rerum Aethiopiarum Scriptores Occidentales Inediti", edit. Beccari,Camilo, 1905-1906, Rome. C.F. B e c k i n g h a m and G.W.B. H u n t i n g f o r d, eds. And extracts are preserved in an old book by Father Francisco Alvares, The Prester John of the Indies; a true relation of the lands of the Prester John, being the narrative of the Portuguese Embassy to Ethiopia in 1520; 2 vols, Hakluyt Society, Cambridge, 1961.
And German extracts are in "Der Dritte Tempel" H. Pfeifer, Vlg. Die Kommenden, Freiburg in Br., 1970.

7 La Vie de Lalibala
This version, preserved in Ge'ez, was translated into French under the title, *La Vie de Lalibala, Roi d' Éthiopie*, by Prof. J. Perruchon. It is not available in English. Its publication details are: La Vie de Lalibala, Roi d' Éthiopie Traduction par Jules

Perruchon, published in 1892, Ernest Leroux editeur, 28 Rue Bonaparte 28 Paris Publications De l'École des Lettres D'Alger Bulletin de Correspondance Africaine.

8 Anna-Lena Röstin, Arvet i Främlingars Hand, Bibeltrogna Vänners Förlag, Stockholm, p. 208.

9 Origenes: Sources Chrétiennes Origène WRIGENOUS TWN EIS TO KATA IWANNHN EUAGGELION EXHGHTIKWN Les Éditions du Cerf, Paris, 1996, Tome 1, 208.

10 Khorshed Nyavis, in The Zend Avesta, part 2, trans. J. Darmesteter, Motilal Banarsidass Delhi, 1981, p. 351

11 Playne ps. 138-139

12 Michael Gervers, in The Rehabilitation Of the Zaguë Kings And The Building Of The Däbrä Sina Golgotha Sellassie Complex In Lalibäla
http://www.wgsr.uw.edu.pl/pub/uploads/ab03/3Gervers.pdf

13 Bianchi Barriviera, mentioned by Michael Gervers, in The Rehabilitation Of the Zaguë Kings And The Building Of The Däbrä Sina

14 R. Grierson & S. Munro-Hay The Ark of the Covenant; the true story of the greatest relic of antiquity, Weidenfeld & Nicholson, London, 1999, p. 252.

15 The Cave of Treasures: The Book of the Cave of Treasures: a History of the Patriarchs and the kings, their successors from the creation to the crucifixion of Christ, trans. E.A. Wallis-Budge, The Religious Tract Society, London, 1927.

16 This document known as Tanasee 90, Rema 1 Bl. 198rb-201rc, is listed in Äthiopische Handschriften vom Tanasee 2, Ernst Hammerschmidt, Franz Steiner Vlg, Wiesbaden, 1977, p. 115.

17 Plutarch, Fragments 178, from Johannes of Stobae, Anthology 4.52.49, in M. Meyer, Ancient Mysteries, edit. M. Meyer, Univ. Penn., Philadelphia, 1986

18 The Egyptian Book of the Dead, trans. E. A. Wallis-Budge, RKP, London, 1869

19 Origenes, see ref. 9, p 142.

20 The Odes to Solomon, in The Lost Books of the Bible, edit. F. Crane, World Publishing Co., Cleveland, 1926 & Die Oden Salomos, trans. W. Bauer, KIT 1963

21 E. A. Wallis-Budge, trans. The Ethiopian Book of Life, (the Lefafa Sedek), AMS Press, New York, 2003.

22 New Testament Apocrypha, edit. W. Schneemelcher, engl. trans. R. Wilson, Vol.1, Westminster Press, Philadelphia, 1963 p. 409

23 Gerster p. 97

24 Dante Alighieri, the Divine Comedy; Hell, Canto 1, trans. Dorothy Sayers, Penguin Books, Harmondsworth, 1974

25 E. A. Wallis-Budge, The Gods of the Egyptians, Vol 2., Dover, N.Y. 1969 p.144

26 The Oxford Classical Dictionary, edits. N. Hammond, H. Scullard, 2nd edit. Clarendon, Oxford, 1976

27 Sylvia Plankhurst, in Ethiopia; A Cultural History, Essex, Lalibela House p.160

28 Playne 129-130

29 Sirach 17:17 [ca. 100 BC], the Targum of Pseudo-Jonathan, 3 Enoch 17:8, 18:2,

30:2 [ca. 500AD] and the Testament of the 12 Patriarchs [ca. 100 BC] Appendix 1, chpt.8:6. These views are embodied in various Jewish writings, see The Legends of the Jews, Vol. 1, p.173 and Vol. 5, p.194

30 Tanasee 91, Rema 2 Bl. 204va. listed in, Äthiopische Handschriften vom Tanasee, 2 Ernst Hammerschmidt, p. 127 & p. 142

31 Tanasee 91, Rema 2 Bl. 204va. listed in, Äthiopische Handschriften vom Tanasee, 2 Ernst Hammerschmidt, p. 119

32 Gospel of Philip, The Nag Hammadi Library in English, J. Robinson (Director of translation project), E.J. Brill, Leiden 1977 p.138

33 Prof. Mark Jarzombek, Lalibela and Libanos; the king and the hydro-engineer of 13th century Ethiopia, (Lalibela and Libanos pdf; Google)

34 The Book of the Dead, trans. Wallis-Budge, Chapters 53, p.196 & chapt. 85, p.273

35 Hastings Encyclopaedia Religion & Ethics, edit. J. Hastings, vol 6, p 488.

36 Stuart Munro-Hay & Pamela Taor, Ethiopia, the Unknown Land, I.B.Tauris, 2002

Other Works Consulted

The Apocrypha and Pseudepigrapha of the Old Testament in English, R. H. Charles, edit, OUP, London, 1978
Michela Gervers: The Rehabilitation Of The Zaguë Kings And The Building Of The Däbrä Sina Golgotha Sellassie Complex In Lalibäla
http://www.wgsr.uw.edu.pl/pub/uploads/ab03/3Gervers.pdf

Illustration Credits

1 The author

2 The author

3 The author

4 From Wikimedia Commons License, CC 3.0 Photographer: Jialiang Gao Jan. 2002. His fine website is: www.peace-on-earth-org. and is about World Photography; an exposition aiming to promote international cultures and understanding by means of photography.

The use by this author of the above photograph does not in any way imply that the photograher shares or supports the views expressed by this author.

5 From Wikimedia Commons GNU License, Photographer: BluesyPete, 26 March 2008

The use by this author of the above photograph does not in any way imply that the photographer shares or supports the views expressed by this author.

6A Ancient coin, not in copyright

6B Wikimedia Commons Photographer: CT Snow, Hsinchu Taiwan, 21 July2006 License CCA 2.

The use by this author of the above photograph does not in any way imply that the photographer shares or supports the views expressed by this author.

7A The author

7B Private photo made available to the author

8 Wikimedia commons Photographer: Giustino Aug 2005
http://flickr.com/photos/giustino /86497274/

The use by this author of the above photograph does not in any way imply that the photographer shares or supports the views expressed by this author.

9 Wikimedia commons both illustrations in the public domain

10 Wikimedia commons Medieval drawing in Biblioteca Apostolica MS latin 4776

11 Wikimedia commons (slightly altered) Photographer: Giustino
http://flickr.com/photos/giustino /38850330/

12 The author

Index

End notes

[i] "Puis Dieu ordonna à l'ange de ramener Lalibala sur la terre et de faire rentrer son âme dans son corps.....qui exécutait l'ordre que Dieu lui avait donné de le ramener dans le corps d'où il l'avait tire."

[ii] See Malcolm Barber, The New Knighthood: a History of the Order of the Temple. Cambridge Uni press, 1995

[iii] Actually, the numbers 70 and 72 are somewhat interchangeable with regard to this theme, some documents say 70, others say 72. The Old Testament mentions that there are 70 nations, and some esoteric Hebrew texts also mention this. However, other esoteric Hebrew texts refer to 72 nations, or 72 languages as the primal template of the groups of people living on the Earth.

[iv] The Greek text here is ambiguous, it might just refer to 70, but 72 is regarded as much more likely.

[v] The treatise is called *The Rehabilitation Of The Zaguë Kings And The Building Of The Däbrä Sina Golgotha Sellassie Complex In Lalibäla*

[vi] About 250 years after the death of Lalibela, the famous Venetian artist Nicolo Brancaleone worked there, and introduced a more naturalistic look to their religious paintings.